Behavioral Strengths and Employment Strategies Augmenting Career Success

Behavioral Strengths and Employment Strategies Augmenting Career Success

Bridging the Best of 2 Worlds

Jim McDonald

∫∆ Integrating Change

authorHOUSE®

AuthorHouse™
1663 Liberty Drive
Bloomington, IN 47403
www.authorhouse.com
Phone: 1 (800) 839-8640

Published by AuthorHouse   11/17/2018

ISBN: 978-1-4817-7654-7 (sc)
ISBN: 978-1-4817-7653-0 (e)

Library of Congress Control Number: 2013912691

Print information available on the last page.

Any people depicted in stock imagery provided by Thinkstock are models,
and such images are being used for illustrative purposes only.
Certain stock imagery © Thinkstock.

This book is printed on acid-free paper.

Because of the dynamic nature of the Internet, any web addresses or links contained in this book may have changed
since publication and may no longer be valid. The views expressed in this work are solely those of the author and do
not necessarily reflect the views of the publisher, and the publisher hereby disclaims any responsibility for them.

CONTENTS

Dedication

I dedicated the first edition of this book to my wife, Ann, my two Step-sons, Stephen and Jim, and, especially my six grandchildren, Matt, Brennah, Owen, Aiden, Grace and Avary.

I wish to dedicate this second edition to my late father and his cousin, Mary. As first cousins, they share their parent's optimism and resilience; two critical behavioral strengths important to personal success. They both believed in leading by example. To this day I miss my Father's calm, understated sense of humor, mixture of rye wit, intelligence, all blended with a touch of sarcasm. With a background in labor law, my father represented those who had little to fall back on; including Delano farm laborers and those he helped who were segregated in off-base housing by the US Military during the Second World War

My father, and my second cousin, Mary, shared values important to me, but none as important as fairness and equity. To these two wonderful people, I dedicate this second edition of Behavioral Strengths and Employment Strategies.

Acknowledgements

First and foremost, thanks again to my wife, Ann, for tolerating my insatiable appetite for the unattainable perfection. In many ways, the first dimension of one's occupational success is defined by five facets of Behavioral Strengths. In retrospect, my motivational style to improve on the first edition is explained by my behavioral strengths which include my sense of optimism that my efforts will help others; by the realization that I am driven by a unique personality:, that I am a product of academic and professional Interests and experience; that my inner sense of Resilience has and will always sustain me through periods of doubt and frustration.

Thanks again to Jack Kuenzel, a long-time friend and Human Resources executive, for his confidence in my experience and dedication to HR. My two close friends, Lorenzo Chambliss, J.D., retired Senior County Counsel, and Dr. Jesus Garcia, Professor of Curriculum and Instruction, continue to amaze me with their contributions. Likewise, Ron Visconti, Director of a large, community-based non-profit organization, and his wife Eve, embody the idea that business and community can make for great partners.

I also wish to recognize those from my alma mater school of Industrial Psychology who have taken the Readiness Profile and provide invaluable feedback. They have helped make the Profile a down-to-earth application of the concepts and two dimensions outlined in the book.

Foreword

∫Δ *Integrating Change*

Occupational success requires putting individual strengths and job strategies together, in a way that maximizes problem solving for change, good ideas and creative solutions. According to Steven Johnson, author of *Where Good Ideas Come From*, when challenges mix with other answers, solutions to problems "converge in some shared physical or intellectual space." (p.163). Similarly, combining your ideas with those in this book, or from others, will combine in solutions totally unexpected to achieving occupational success.

Based on over forty years of corporate and consulting experience, it is my conviction that deliberately combining your inherent behavioral strengths with smart, occupational strategies will greatly improve your chances of achieving lifelong occupational satisfaction and success.

Introduction

Behavioral Strengths and Employment Strategies: a Tactical Approach to Career Success

Behavioral Strengths and Employment Strategies **rests on the notion that occupational success is best achieved by using a combination of individual strengths and smart, practical employment strategies**. The premise is that individual strengths and employment strategies overlap, like a thatched roof in a storm, protecting its owner from adversity. Strengths and strategies bond and influence each other in the form of a dynamic system, designed to be fluid and reactive in a world of work in constant motion.

Power of Self: Five Behavioral Dimensions

Optimism	Personality	Interests	Experience	Resilience
Positive outlook for future employment	Our internal and external image	Drive to explore, learn, and discover	Everything, work and otherwise	Capacity to overcome adversity and rejection

Occupational Solutions: Five Employment Strategies

Action	Research	Resumes	Interviews	Negotiation
From introspection to motion	Connecting interests and resources	Personality, interests, and experience	Meetings with employers, and others	Needs and Offers

☑ Behavioral Strengths

Career development include five personal strengths: **Optimism, Personality, Interests, Experience, and Resilience. When** combined, the five Behavioral Strengths represent our potential to meet the challenges of career and occupational development.

☑ Strengths and Strategies in Motion

Competing in today's job market requires the skill to convince employers that you have what it takes to do the job. In addition to compelling resumes, and eye-catching correspondence, today's job market requires facility with the Internet, membership in one or more social networks, and a practical understanding of employer resume retrieval systems.

Given the current labor market, even a little frustration and rejection can set the strongest of us back on our heels. **If so, how about trying another approach? How about considering a balanced approach to occupational strategies?** I am not suggesting a 360-degree change in direction, just one that considers viewing one's mission from another perspective. If improving your resume or interviewing technique has not helped, consider other strategies, a reassessment, of your current position. Even a modest shift in career strategies, such as taking another, close examination of your work contributions, can make the world of work seem a lot more inviting.

- **The Readiness Profile (Appendix A)**

Knowing when, where, and how to start any project is said to be half the battle. Whether building a house, or a project to gain reemployment, getting a sense of when, where or how to start or restart the process is tantamount to success. To that end, **the "Readiness Profile," designed to help you set a starting point from which to progress.**

- **Merging the Best of Strengths with Smart Employment Strategies**

Whereas Optimism can have a tremendous influence on Action, Personality can do the same for an Interview. Individual Strengths, such as Optimism and Personality, influence the kinds of occupational strategies we favor when job hunting or career building. In the same way that the strength of one's personality can influence the outcome of a job interview, or the look and feel of a resume, when strengths guide strategies, the outcome can be a lifetime of occupational success.

- **Untapped Potential**

Like a vast natural resource buried beneath the tundra, individual strengths often lay dormant, until pushed to the surface by adversity, such as an unexpected job loss. In spite of the trauma of a job loss or abrupt change in one's career, taking cover with a sense of your internal strengths and solid employment strategies will overcome adversity. However, if there is anything good to be said about adversity, it is that it often leads to greater opportunities and success. It may sound trite, but trading adversity for occupational growth is a far better path to long-term success than accepting defeat.

$\int\Delta$ *Integrating Change*

CHAPTER ONE

OPTIMISM

Anticipating Success

"I Think I Can, I Think I Can" [1941. The Little Engine That Could]

Darwin and Edison

Some of the brightest and most creative minds exude optimism. His teachers told Thomas Edison, inventor of the ubiquitous light bulb, that he was "*too stupid to learn anything*." His early work resume was not much better, Edison was "released" from his first two jobs for being "*non-productive*." On the other hand, Edison excelled as a committed inventor, a career where he mixed optimism with perseverance. Although Edison might have been discouraged after a thousand or so experiments, he electrified the world with the light bulb. When a reporter asked Edison, "*How did it feel to fail 1,000 times?*" Edison quipped, "*I didn't fail 1,000 times; the light bulb was an invention with 1,000 steps.*" Although it took over a 1,000 "failures," **Thomas Edison turned optimism into one of the greatest inventions of all time. Similarly, Charles Darwin, another pioneer into the nature of science, put the notion of evolution into virtually every science book**. Like Edison, Darwin's sense of optimism and perseverance as a researcher that drove him to articulate the science of evolution. Darwin admits in his autobiography that he "*was considered by all (his) masters and father, (to be) a very ordinary boy, rather below the common standard of intellect.*" Darwin resisted his father's insistence he become a physician Instead, Darwin chose the career as a researcher. Darwin confessed that if it were not for his sense of optimism, he would not have lived out his dreams as a researcher. If it were not for their sense of optimism, Edison's invention, and Darwin's theories might still be on the workbench.

☑ Importance of Optimism

Why is a positive outlook important to occupational success? Because lack of optimism will create a whole slew of problems, most of them transitory, but some more serious, such as depression and feelings of hopelessness. Optimism is the reason we take action to proceed, take risks and accept failure as a normal part of life. Nevertheless, even when one's outlook for the future is low, there are practical measures to ways to improve one's sense of optimism. Like a water pump, one can prime a sense of optimism by visualizing positive outcomes. Imagine winning the lottery.

Optimistic visualizations can work, but a better way to gin up optimism is to take a step or two into action. **The sheer power of action, even the smallest, can have a wonderful effect on one's outlook**. You can think about optimism, or you take steps to put yourself into first gear and motion. Either way will work.

- **Research**

Research shows that a positive outlook helps overcome many obstacles. Employees who report a sense of optimism, for example, use more problem-solving strategies compared to their pessimistic peers (Strutton, D., and J. Lumpkin 1995). Moreover, problem-solving skills are like gold to most employers. In another study, participants who felt positive about their futures reported more success in solving work-related problems (Norman P., S. Collins, M. Conner, and R. Martin. 1995). Studies conducted in academic settings have established a strong relationship between optimism and performance (Aspinwall, L.G. and S.E. Taylor, 1992). **In other words, optimism influences performance at work, in sports, or in the search for occupational success**.

☑ Trends

Conrad Schmidt, of the Corporate Leadership Counsel, concluded in 2010 that layoffs had gradually stabilized, that more workers had resigned than were laid off. Prior to April 2010, layoffs exceeded resignations. A good sign? Yes. In today's economy, it appears several labor market forces are counteracting the "Great Jobs Recession." What are they?

- **Executive Turnover**

More executive-level employees report they are more optimistic about leaving their employers to pursue "greener pastures." Harvard Business Review stated in May 2010, that 25 percent of "top performers" planned to leave their employers for "greener pastures." This finding contrasted with the same period in 2006, where only 10% of top performers reported their intent to explore other opportunities with greater challenges and rewards, not out of fear or need, but more out of a greater sense of optimism for the future. Where executives go, so goes the mandate to increase sales and income, or the need to ramp up manufacturing and expand hiring. To an executive, the opportunity to hire more staff, increase corporate profits, corporate growth, greater recognition, pay, stock options, and performance bonuses, translate into more recruiting and employment for others. The current labor market remains anemic, but there are definite signs of life and optimism.

- **Labor Turnover**

Turnover, or the rate at which employees need replacing, may run as high as ten or more percent in good times. However, in tougher times, such as those created by the "Great Recession," turnover is often much lower, by quite a bit, somewhere around three percent. This means employees are staying put. **Although meager, any turnover, even one percent, is good for job seekers. It means jobs are coming available, creating more potential opportunities.** In the 1980s, ten percent turnover was common. A company with 1,000 employees, for example, with 10% turnover would need to replace 100 employees to stay even. This does not mean that exactly the same jobs were replaced; only that openings were being created. **Unless a company's turnover is zero, which is highly unlikely, there will always be job opportunities for persistent applicants.**

- **The Hidden Job Market**

Roughly eighty percent of all jobs filled go unadvertised. Even in this deep recession, the number of jobs filled each month number in the tens of thousands. For every job posted online or in newspapers, seven to ten more go unadvertised. The hidden job market is alive and well. The hidden job market represents jobs filled by more informal methods, such as "word-of-mouth," or by unsolicited inquiries, or by referrals to hiring managers.

- **Below the Surface**

Don't believe everything you read, especially if all you read about jobs is in the help-wanted pages or online. If what you see about job openings is small, it could be that what you see is only the tip of the iceberg. **A better way to look for hidden jobs below the surface is to look for changing business conditions**. This may take a bit of research, but acquisitions of other companies, divestitures of divisions, reports of reorganizations, consolidations, or relocations indicate change and, therefore, the need for more or different employees. Furthermore, inside, away from view of the outside world, and behind the personnel "curtain," other changes are taking place, including retirements, promotions, voluntary and involuntary terminations, transfers, and resignations. **Every day and every hour, like one's heartbeat, a tremendous amount of activity is taking place behind the walls of an employer's façade**. Those seeking new opportunities should relish the fact that business change is creating opportunities, that business change is normal, expected, but obscured from view by the job market.

- **Technological Demand**

Technological change drives companies into new products and services, which often results in labor market demand for new employees. Hardly a day goes by without a major media story featuring massive changes to business and corporations. Consider Apple, Kodak, HP, Facebook, or Salesforce.com to name a few that have undergone tremendous changes, which creates demand for new skills and experience, of all kinds and at all levels. However, the sword of change cuts in both directions, for and against the labor market. On one hand, change creates new jobs and new career opportunities, yet imposes expectations that the workforce and applicant pool be ready to step into new and challenging jobs. At least be ready to be trained in new technologies.

- **Skills Vacuum**

Financial columnist, Tapan Munroe believes that a national skill shortage has created what he calls the "job gap," in other words, a lack of trained, qualified applicants. In the book, *Closing America's Job Gap* (www.ClosingAmericasjobgap.com), Munroe and his colleagues note that the skills vacuum will be America's number one challenge for years to come. Munroe sees innovation and technology as having created a temporary, if not significant, vacuum for trained US workers. Most economists agree. The skills vacuum is a positive but troubling sign for the unemployed. Munroe identified ten employment sectors having an unfilled demand for trained workers including green energy jobs, embedded engineering applications, and industrial robotics. You, the reader, should know that opportunities exist, but are you ready to compete for them? If not, are you optimistic enough to make an investment in more education and training?

☑ **Economic Winds**

Granted, optimism is difficult to define, and harder yet to put in plain words. Optimism is a confluence of positive emotional and physical sensations. It is the kind of emotion that floats, up and down, like the stock market or interest rates-positive one moment, and negative the next. However, if you want that tingling sensation it is hard to beat the rewards from feeling optimistic. When you feel that sense of self-confidence, self-assurance, and invincibility that comes from success you are in the zone of optimism. **In my opinion, on the scale of euphoria, optimism ranks a ten. Why so high? Because optimism fuels action, and vice versa.**

Optimism is a powerful motivator. Not to recognize optimism's influence is to deny its importance in achieving success. Even small amount of optimism can get a person to make that first step toward positive change. Lao-Tzu, 600 BC, founder of the Chinese philosophy, Taoism, wrote that even the longest journey would start with a single step. The first step then is to examine the economy for signs of job growth, as modest as they may be, for sparks of optimism and challenge. As it turns out, there are a number of signs that our economy is not completely flat on its back.

- **Effects of the 2009 Stimulus**

According to Pew Charitable Trusts (www.pewtrusts.org), the Stimulus Program consisted of $787 billion Although not as great as some economists felt it should be, the 2009 stimulus package injected billions of dollars into various sectors of the economy, roughly half into the American Recovery and Reinvestment Act. Arguments, pro and con, continue to dominate political and economic discussions. Most economists, such as Nobel Laureate, Paul Krugman, would say that the Stimulus continues to have a positive, even if limited, effect on employment. Eleven billion dollars went to construction and renewable energy jobs. Injecting billions of stimulus dollars helped to side-step the on-rush of a severe recession, but not enough to soften the blow to millions trying to regain economic footing.

- **Labor Market Demand**

Employment changes because of numerous economic forces, including those affecting specific industries, along with technical innovation. National labor market demand has been slowly, but sporadically improving, creating a seesaw graph of job growth. Most jobs are filled on a "just in time" or on an "as needed" basis. When weather slams large populations, FEMA (Federal Emergency Management Agency) goes into action, placing hundreds of workers on field assignments. Demand, at the national level, or for the local mom and pop store, can turn on a dime. The task is to remain alert to changes in sectors of the labor market of interest to you. **Accepting global macro-level generalizations as gospel often overstates the complexities at the level of the local job market**.

Those employed may dismiss bad news, whereas an unemployed worker may feel, deep down, that the job market is "terrible." The truth is often somewhere in between.

☑ Labor Forecasts

- **US Bureau of Labor Statistics**

The September 2015 unemployment rate remains at or around 5.1 %, the lowest since 2008. Granted, labor market numbers never stay constant but a recent BLS job growth by industry reports says the health sector led the way in terms of job growth. In an economy where new jobs are coming from lower-pay positions like health, instead of better-pay positions like manufacturing, wage growth will continue to remain anemic. The economy continues to add around 100,000 jobs per month, not fantastic, but not horrible.

- **Moody's Outlook**

In 2013, Moody's *economy.com* foresaw a payroll decline through mid-2010, and that construction, particularly home construction, and manufacturing would improve first. Although infra structure construction continues to lag, auto manufacturing, on the other hand, is doing well.

☑ Networking Success

Studies show that trust underpins a sense of optimism (*Scheier, M.F., and C.S. Carver. 1985; Strutton, D., and J. Lumpkin. 1992*). **A number of strategies enhance optimism, but one of the best is to engage with those closest to you, in other words, family, friends, and colleagues.**

- **Friends and Colleagues**

The first line of defense against loneliness and frustration is to stay in contact with family, friends, and colleagues. Relying on friends and colleagues for job leads may feel like an imposition, but do not underestimate their willingness to at least express support. Although you feel a little awkward at first, ask for support. Try to stay positive and upbeat with those in your circle of contacts, past and present. Former colleagues are often willing to help, for several reasons, one being human nature. It is a well-known fact that colleagues and peers who retain their jobs, when at the same time, their friends lose theirs, often feel a sense of guilt at being retained. **Whether out of a sense of guilt or genuine empathy, former colleagues will be happy to provide moral support and referrals to**

other opportunities. They themselves may be looking for other opportunities, and be concerned for their own security. Another reason for staying in contact with former colleagues is another human condition nature—emotional health.

- **Employee Referrals**

Most hiring results from the grapevine: from informal contacts, word of mouth, referrals, friends, former colleagues, or prior supervisors. Jobs filled through informal networking confirm the phrase, the "hidden job market." Informal networks are a great source of jobs sheltered from the public eye, jobs not advertised, but, nonetheless, open and active. Most large employers (5,000 or more employees) promote employee referral programs with cash incentives to encourage employees to refer candidates for hard-to-fill openings. Those referred generally make good employees. Pursuing the "hidden job market" is far less an act of faith than it is fact and reality. Pursuing jobs in the "hidden" market is a very effective, if not the best way to secure reemployment. I know it for a fact because my studies constantly verified employee referrals as the greatest source for new employees.

- **Person-to-Person**

Internet social networking has changed the game with respect to job and career management. In today's jargon, networks and networking refer to communication between computers. **Networking, on the other hand, has a dual meaning, the second referring to person-to-person communication, either face-to-face or by social networking over computers.** Networking, in all its forms, is the gateway to employment, and one of the most effective communication techniques referred to in the vernacular as, "cold calling."

- **Person-to-Employers**

If you decide to try cold calling to potential employers, be prepared to deal with automated, voice recognition systems, a significant screen to person-to-person communication. They are as common as the telephone, but universally annoying. Start with a list of potential employers.

There are various ways of contacting employers, but for starters call the company receptionist or Human Resources department. Take a more bold approach: call managers directly. Whomever you choose to call, begin first by "practicing" a few "throw away" calls of little consequence to your job search. However, before calling, have a plan. Know how to address the person who answers your call. Anticipate the conversation. Skilled use of the telephone takes practice, not unlike calling for a date. The dreaded "brush off" has stopped many potential job candidates. The objective may be different, but calls to an employer or to a romantic interest share a common denominator: they both involve possible rejection. **However, you can overcome some of the fear by having several good questions handy**. Good questions convey knowledge of an employer's business, and your credibility. It will help to prepare a brief script (tailored to the person you are calling) with points you want to make, and questions you want to ask. In addition, have a calendar ready in order to make an appointment if necessary. If you have access to the Internet, open the company web site. A little practice will eventually increase your sense of confidence and reduce your anxiety.

- **Telephone Confidence**

If the fear of rejection has you in a bind, try taking small steps to build your self-confidence. You might try calling a company and asking for the name of the Human Resources representative responsible for recruiting. Consider making for five or so contacts. Your phone anxiety should decrease. Little by little, the anxiety of calling will get easier. Vary your approach a bit. Try different kinds and sizes of companies. Note your sense of progress with difficult calls. Develop alternative introductions. Be an applicant on one call and a referral from a career-networking group on the other. The more you practice, the greater your sensitivity will be to any indications of encouragement. **Keep in mind the fact that calling and communicating with strangers is a skill, and skills can get better with practice**.

- **Mutual Support**

Sharing interests and experience with others improves one's sense of optimism. Richard Bolles (*jobhuntersbible.com*), author of several well-known career development books, cites the following: "*Research shows that people who attend job support groups have a 90% greater likelihood of finding gainful employment in less than 3 months, than those who do not.*" **It is generally accepted that networking with others enhances optimism and the ability to confront and manage change, instead of resisting it.**

- **Community Support**

There are many sources for employment support, but one of the best is the community non-profit agency. Community agencies often provide job placement assistance to job seekers as well as helping employers find good employees. **Because community agencies work with local employers, many act as transition conduits to those looking for employment.**

Most cities have public employment centers that offer extensive information and the opportunity to network with others in the same boat. Many secular and religious centers offer support and office space to those interested in transition networking. Meeting with others provides a chance to discuss and share frustrations, successes, and failures. Ultimately, networking with others offers the chance to share experiences, job openings, and leads, all of which helps attain and maintain much-needed optimism.

☑ Networking Missteps

The simplest communication techniques can help build and cement relationships. For example, staying attentive and focused during a conversation will reinforce two-way communications. **Enthusiastically accepting suggestions, advice, or opinions is as good as mining gold.** Most networking communication comes naturally, but sometimes-networking mishaps do happen. For example, it is easy to forget to thank a contact for their time and interest in your search. Nevertheless, these are the mishaps to avoid.

- **Presumptive Permission**

Do not forget to ask permission if you can use the name of the person giving you a referral. Referrals are precious. Likewise, be sure to reciprocate with an offer to assist return the favor. Simple courtesies are anything but simple when networking with others.

- **Acting Desperate**

Avoid acting desperate (in spite of what the truth may be) when asked what you do for work; avoid jumping in to state your desperate need for work. Instead, answer with a brief overview of your background, something like the summary used in an email or in your resume. Emphasize, instead, your desire to join a team, to learn new systems and to contribute.

☑ Building Optimism

- **Self-fulfilling Prophecy**

Success depends, in large measure, on how optimistic you feel about your future success. If you see the market as tight (that there are few jobs out there for you), you run the risk of generating a negative self-fulfilling prophecy, the kind that impedes success. Negative or positive perceptions of the job market can lead to inevitable self-fulfilling prophecies. If you see the job market as bright, you will spend more time and energy looking. Admittedly, the job market is bad, but try not to let the obvious become a negative self-fulfilling prophesy. Collect positive signs of opportunities, and scrap the negative.

- **Outside One's Comfort Zone**

Taking risks may seem counterproductive to career transition, but modest risks have their own rewards. A few such modest risks include optimism, self-confidence, and assurance. To gauge your tolerance for risk, first determine your comfort zone. Note which social activities you feel confident about, like conversing with friends, taking excursions, or night classes. Next, consider activities you try to avoid, those that make you feel uncomfortable undertaking, such as cold calling.

Anticipation of a rude administrator may seem minor to some, but an obstacle to others. Regardless of the anticipated reaction, job seekers often have to take risks, face the rude administrator, and or engage with strangers and interview with people who have control over their futures. Who enjoys denial and rejection, even by email? Nevertheless, until we find another universe, in our interaction with others, we will always face the possibility of rejection, especially from an interview.

How about out-of-the-area travel to meet with an employer? Once you have developed an idea where your comfort zone begins and ends, you can proceed to activities you feel most comfortable with, and test the waters related to those activates that are uncomfortable. You may not be able to change, to any degree, the uncomfortable side of risk, but there are a number of ways to reduce the sting. Practice, knowledge, and new strategies will help. **Taking even modest risks to increase exposure to others who may have opportunities will lead to greater inner sense of confidence and optimism.**

- **Rebalance Old Ideas**

We alone control our optimism. There are steps you can take to improve a sense of optimism, even modest ones. Attending workshops can improve a sense of connectedness. The local library often conducts seminars and workshops. Simply expressing one's interests and experience with others improves a sense of self-esteem and confidence. Serendipity works best in these cauldrons of communications, often producing referrals to employers actively recruiting.

- **Consider New Strategies**

Fear of taking risks is normal, but the benefits of taking some risks to explore new strategies far outweigh upsetting our comfort zone. For example, joining a transition-networking group involves some stress: meeting new contacts, encountering different personalities and sharing feelings. One of the basic fears is appearing different or out of step. Consider the potential benefits. Simply listening to a speaker from a local company may provide an occupational connection. The opportunity to do a mock video interview, or to role-play an applicant, may not be the Actors' Studio, but, in some ways, it may be better. Practicing how to ask questions about pay and benefits may make you feel like a seasoned pro.

- **Exploring Smaller Companies**

It takes each of us to ponder how to master the job market, to search for signs of occupational growth and opportunity. Before discounting job opportunities all together, examine healthcare, electronics, or office automation, for hidden opportunities. Many smaller companies, for example, do not require a college degree. Remain flexible. Smaller companies are more often turning to temporary help agencies to ride out the lack of certainty or a tighter labor market. Wrapping experience with a willingness to be flexible for an interim period may be a hop, skip, and a jump away from full employment.

- **Give Yourself a Lift: Update the Resume**

Who thinks her or his resume is perfect or even strong enough to convince an employer to take a second look? Even a slight change to your contributions, or the use of stronger action words, will improve a resume. **What kind of impression are you trying to convey to an employer? Does your personality come through? Have you clearly stated your interests?** Have you added new classes to your resume? No matter how limited your experience or impressive a work history, every resume can be enhanced. Not only will rewriting sections of your resume strengthen it, but also the exercise will reinforce your sense of accomplishment. Remember, a compelling, well-written resume goes a long way with employers.

- **Accept Imperfection**

Most of us will never find that perfect job. However, in absence of perfection, some level of flexibility and compromise will help broaden your outlook of potential opportunities. **Jobs not perfectly in line with our career goals may offer other avenues to additional opportunities.** If you have to set aside your occupational goals, continue to look for educational opportunities. As a rule, try to continue adding new skills, particularly technical and computer skills. They are tantamount to staying in sync with the ever-changing world of work. Whether you use this book or some other to inspire personal change is not the point. What does matter is that you take charge of your own occupational destiny, be it rocky or smooth. Remember: there is no perfection

☑ A Brighter Future

Accentuate the Positive (Johnny Mercer, 1944). Calamity and despair gripped the nation's mood with news of the attack on Pearl Harbor in 1941. Johnny Mercer, iconic musician and songwriter, wrote a song that inspired millions of listeners to reach for a nation's collective sense of optimism. Reflecting our nation's resolve to remain positive, his lyrics expressed a simple, but monumental truth: that a spirit of optimism is capable of immense power and sustenance in the face of adversity.

Today, few people are lucky enough to pursue careers that become stable over five to 10 years. Furthermore, fewer, if any, educational programs prepare students for any particular long-term career. Whereas we might have to sacrifice stability, we will replace it with more fluidity, benefits that are more portable, and more opportunities to be competitive in the workplace. For instance, our ability to create new technologies, improve methods and systems, and create new businesses, bodes well for the future. **As industrial and information technologies continue to change, occupations and careers will also change, creating greater employment demands and opportunities in the market place.**

CHAPTER TWO
PERSONALITY

Persona

I marvel how Nature could ever find space For so many strange contrasts in one human face: There's thought and no thought, and there's paleness and bloom And bustle and sluggishness, pleasure and gloom.["A Character" by William Wordsworth Longfellow]

Personality

Beginning with the advent of human consciousness, personality has inspired philosophers, writers, poets, playwrights, and research psychologists to explore the nature and strength of personality. From the beginning of human time, personality has been a subject of interest and intrigue, like the beguiling smile on the Mona Lisa. What personality lies behind that smile? What predispositions, prejudices, emotions, preferences, fears, and insecurities does that smile hide? Personality is not something we dwell on, that is, until one wonders naively what they could have done to overcome that important job interview. When we have recounted experience and interests, our attention invariably turns to personality, over and over, like a bad movie, in search of the plot we know is submerged somewhere in the personality of the main character. In reality, most of us float through life, oblivious of the force our personalities can have on others, and on ourselves. Certainly imperfect, largely immutable, yet unavoidable, personality moves us through life's oceans, like icebergs, submerged below the surface, mostly unseen by others, but, like an iceberg, our personalities are capable of immense power.

Derived from the Latin "persona," originally referred to as a theatrical mask, later, between the 9th and 6th centuries BC, the Greeks expanded persona to include performance. Maybe a stretch, but in many ways, we all perform as if we are on stage, playing opposite others, in all sorts of dramas, comedies, or romances, employment interviews or during offer negotiations. Whether one is outgoing or passive, one's personality plays an integral role in occupational success.

☑ Murphy's Biosocial Theory of Personality

According to Gardner Murphy, eminent social psychologist, we act as biosocial creatures, traversing the world of people, places, and things, collecting experience, like human honeybees, sharing ideas, inspiration, and wisdom, as we go. Unlike the honeybee on a singular mission, we human creatures follow a much more complicated GPS than the one in our car. In our quest for success, we use an internal sense of optimism and affirmation to guide our personalities, interests, and experience toward success.

Murphy theorized about the symbiotic relationship between our inner, bio-psychological world, and the outer, social-physical world. Hall and Lindzey, In their text book, *Personality Theory*, describe Murphy's biosocial creature *"as a biological organism, designed by nature to maintain a reciprocal relationship with its material and social environments"* (p 506). Murphy's model of human behavior serves as this backdrop to this book.

Whereas the five individual strengths in this book link with Murphy's bio-psychological world, the five Occupational Strategies represent Murphy's "social environment." We use our inner bio-psychological strengths to map our direction, whereas we use practical career search tools, such as planning, resume development, and research to take us to our destinations.

- **Public Persona**

Everyone has one—a public persona—our public persona. Personality is our outward display of emotions, feelings, and mannerisms. **Like snowflakes or the rotating image in a kaleidoscope, there are no two copies of any one's personality**. Even identical twins have subtle differences when it comes to their personalities. Unbridled assertiveness, for example, is an asset in a boxing ring, but a turnoff to most hiring managers. Appearing assertive and controlling will impress the police commissioner, but probably not the non-profit director of a children's center. On the other hand, presenting an attentive, open demeanor, will. An applicant with a positive, optimistic outlook with good listening skills, or an engaging demeanor or smile, will engender greater attention and acceptance from others—the kind of attention you want from a hiring manager.

☑ A Personal Companion

Our personalities go where we go. They can take you to places of grandeur, success, and intrigue or lead one to failure and pessimism. Our personalities can take us to places beyond our wildest imaginations, to insights that enhance well-being, or block us from overcoming failure. Nevertheless, one thing is for certain, no personality is perfect, far from it.

Accepting the premise that none of us has a perfect personality is fundamental to managing change and achievement. Accepting that we are all imperfect involves an acceptance of our strengths and weaknesses. Realizing that personality can play a critical role in occupational success is the first step. For most of us, we rarely use our personalities to capacity. Like metals and stripes on a war hero's vest, or on an Olympic champion's shoulder, our personalities are capable of commanding respect and attention, the kind that can convince an employer you are the best of the lot.

☑ The Bio Persona

In today's media, health and personality are ubiquitous. The stakes mean billions of dollars in revenue, for the entertainment and pharmaceutical industries. The emphasis on health and personality affects virtually every segment of our lives, from pain relief and sexual vitality, to our insecurities about our occupational future. Trying to discern the difference between the health/personality duality is like trying to answer the age-old question of what came first—the chicken or the egg. It does not matter. They lace together, not only in concept but also in reality, in plain view under one circumstance and hidden from view in another. One's personality may be perfect for a particular job but, because of an obvious health condition, such as color blindness, access to certain jobs may be restricted. **Health and personality are interwoven so tightly that it is difficult to tell on the surface which one is dominant**. However, over time, most of us will migrate toward jobs and occupations that favor one over the other. **Unlike the perfect balance symbolized by the Chinese Tao, either health or personality will gradually come to dominate job direction and the type of occupation we pursue.**

☑ Personality Type

Personality is a composite of individual biological and social components—seen, felt, and experienced—universal to all, yet uniquely personal. Test specialists spend careers pondering the design, and application of various tests in order to measure the biological, sociological, and psychological components of personality.

One commonly accepted and highly respected personality test is John Holland's *Self-Directed Search.* Included is the *Six Factor Typology*, which states, "The choice of a vocation is an expression of personality." Holland links six personality types to various occupations. Holland's typology has been adopted by the US Department of Labor to describe the personality features of some eight hundred jobs.

☑ Occupational Predisposition

It makes sense to have a reasonably good idea how your personality has influenced your job and career choices. **Studies have shown, for example, that particular occupations attract particular personality types**. "Extroverted" or "outgoing" personalities, for example, appear to favor occupations that require sales and marketing skills, jobs that require good communication skills. Matchups between personality types and job satisfaction are well established. Career specialists use the results of these studies to guide their clients through thorny job and career issues.

- **Holland's Six-Factor Typology**

Personality Type	Tendencies	Occupations
Realistic	practical, asocial, genuine, hardheaded, materialistic, thrifty, persistent, uninvolved	HVAC mechanic, electrical and electronic technicians
Investigative	analytical, intellectual, scientific, explorative, critical, rational, reserved	Computer analyst, medical lab technicians
Artistic	creative, original, independent, cautious, imaginative, impulsive, intuitive, nonconforming, sensitive	Architects, designers
Social	cooperative, supportive, healing, nurturing, patient, kind, friendly, helpful, empathic, tactful	Teachers, home health aids
Enterprising	leader, persuasive, energetic, extraverted, flirtatious, optimistic, self-confident, talkative, aggressive	Lawyers, financial analysts
Conventional	detail-oriented, organized, controlling, careful, inflexible, inhibited, persistent, methodical	Accountants, bank tellers

Table adapted from the Occupational Finder (Revised 1970, 1972, 1974, 1977, 1978), Making Vocational Choices, Second Edition, A Theory of Vocational Personalities, and Work Environments, 1992, Psychological Assessment Resources, Inc., Odessa, FL.

- **Myers-Briggs Type Indicator (MBTI)**

The Meyers-Briggs Type Indicator, a self-administered test, is popular with the public, in spite of its relative complexity. Nevertheless, because the MBTI is somewhat complex, it is best to have an experienced interpreter explain the results. The MTBI pairs sixteen type indicators into "opposing inclinations," such as, "EI, Extroversion-Introversion." The MBTI yields 16 combinations of four different indicators. One of the test's benefits is that profiles can be compared with others working in specific occupations. Because the Type Indicator is highly structured, there is a tendency to treat profile scores as first-person, personality types. "I am an ESTJ, what are you?" Always remember, though, that test scores and profiles are only abstractions of the test taker.

- **The Johari Window**

If possession is 9/10 of the law, then perception is 9/10 of reality. Before Facebook was a scribble, another view of personality was developed in the 1950s by Joseph Luft and Harrington Ingram, Psychology professors at San Francisco State University. The beauty of the Johori Window is its practicality. The model is comprised of two levels of perception: self-perception and perception of self by others. This simple, but elegant model of personality produces a four-quadrant "window." Quadrant one, for example, is identified as the Public Arena, the product of perceptions "Known to Self" and "Known to Others." In other words, others also know what we know of ourselves. Luft and Ingram considered the Public Arena the ideal communication style.

Personality	Known to Others	Unknown to Others
Known to Self	Public Arena	Private Arena
Unknown to Self	Hidden Arena	Unknown Arena

The Johari Model is adapted from Group Process: An Introduction to Group Dynamics by Joseph Luft, Mayfield Publishing Co., 1984.

The second quadrant, for example, is known as the *Hidden Arena*, an area of one's self that is "Unknown to Self," but "Known to Others." The dichotomy in perception defines the "difference of opinion." Take, for example, the grade school teacher who sees herself as firm, yet fair, whereas the Principal sees her as overly strict, impatient and emotionally distant. The model suggests that if the teacher and the principal were to express their differences in perceptions openly, the process would begin to take on the quality of communications described by the Public Arena. The Importance of *Public Arena* communication is that it represents mutual trust, acceptance, and understanding. By the way, this is the kind of communication that leads to successful job interviews.

☑ Skills, Aptitudes, and Competencies

Skill, aptitude, and competency tests range from eye-hand coordination to the Wechsler Adult Intelligence Scale (WAIS), and are instrumental in achieving job and career selection and future occupational success. To that end, the US Government has spent a good deal of time and resources developing tests that help select applicants for the military and for other government agencies.

- **U.S. General Aptitude Test Battery (GATB)**

The self-administered GATB measures general ability, manual dexterity, verbal, numerical, perceptual, and spatial aptitudes. It matches scores from the Occupational Aptitude Survey and Interest Schedule with twelve interest measures that relate to the GATB.

- **U.S. Armed Services Vocational Aptitude Battery (ASVAB)**

The U.S. Army has spent millions of dollars on research and development of the ASVAB, a comprehensive test administered to hundreds of thousands of incoming recruits. The VAB measures personality types and their relationship to jobs in the military.

☑ Tests, Scores, and Practitioners

Personality tests, although very important, are but one measure of our biosocial strengths. As such, they are not to be feared, nor accepted as absolute truth, but, instead, are simply an indicator of occupational direction.

- **Developed by Humans for Humans**

Test scores are simply inferred or abstracted measures of human behavior. In other words, we are not our test scores. Personality profiles are simply byproducts of scores, inferences, and test definitions created by test constructors. Tests designed to measure "intelligence" or "persistence," for example, might use a variety of behaviors to reflect qualities, identified as persistence. Whatever test items psychometrists use to measure qualities such as intelligence or persistence, we humans are the ones who design them. The real beauty is in the comparison of individual personality scores with group profiles. This is where definitions of personality emerge. If asked, how would you define your personality? "Shy," "gregarious," "persistent," "talkative," "even-tempered," "intelligent," "quiet," "studious," "vivacious," "analytical?"

- **Statistical Measures: Validity and Reliability**

Validity and reliability measure a test's utility. Both measures result from rigorous statistical analysis. A test is considered valid when for example, it's criterion, "friendship," correlates significantly with other similar tests measuring "friendship." Validity addresses whether or not a test measures what it purports to measure. Measures of reliability address whether or not the test produces the same or similar results, over time, between similar test groups. For a technical review of one popular test, the FIRO-B, go to https://www.cpp.com/products/index.aspx.

- **Psychometrists**

It is hard to understand the concept of personality without knowing something about psychometrics, the science of test development. The results from test development and their application provide a better understanding of how personality is associated with occupational success, for businesses, counselors, and above all, for individuals.

- **Psychologists**

Whereas psychometrists develop tests, industrial psychologists apply them in different ways and in different settings. One of my former employers, for example, used several psychologists to assess executive-level applicants and employees for promotion.

- **Counselors**

To ensure that tests are properly used, professional associations have established standards and guidelines. The California Association for Counseling and Development (CACD.org), for example, promotes standards for career guidance counselors. As a rule, experienced career counselors should have at least five years of career counseling experience, preferable with a background in business and human resources. At the national level, the American Psychological Association (APA.org) sets rigorous standards for test developers, and counselors. Equivalent to the FDA (Federal Drug Administration), the APA is the watchdog over the development of ethical, accurate tests.

- **Non-judgmental**

Ratings or scores on any test measure are simply scores. Scores are neither right nor wrong, good nor bad, winner nor loser. They are impartial, simply numerical measures that purport only to measure global impressions. When compared to others taking similar tests, results may indicate the strength on some value, such as an inclination toward teamwork, which, may or may not be helpful to the test administrator or individual, depending on results needed. Basketball teams require strong teamwork, whereas inventors may not need to be team-oriented.

- **No Perfection**

In spite of rigorous methodologies and impressive levels of validity and reliability, there are no perfect tests, in that there are no perfect human beings. Personality theories and test scores aside, you and I know intuitively that personality has to be an important component of achieving occupational success. As good as some tests are, we are much more complicated than a simple test score or profile. On the other hand, however, knowing preferred styles of communication, intellectual strengths, or interpersonal weakness, will enable one to make better occupational decisions.

- **Nonsense for Sale**

Whereas practitioners apply psychometric methods to ensure that their tests are valid and reliable, less ethical vendors promote tests that are the equivalent to junk science. Legitimate test design requires strict psychometric methods, extensive quantitative analysis, and peer reviews before being used by the public. Junk tests may appear legitimate on the surface, but, as adage goes, "appearances can be deceiving." Many tests sound and look professional, and may profess to measure everything and anything, from romantic compatibility to artistic ability, but, in reality, are simply designed to exploit the user's naiveté and pocketbook. However, in the light of day, these sub-par tests fail to measure what they purport to measure. Half-baked claims can be potentially harmful. In the hands of the wrong person, meaningless test scores can put a user steps away from an emotional cliff.

☑ Self below the Surface

Unlike the skin-deep effects from a Botox or liposuction procedure, personality below the surface is more difficult to change. We are who we are, as the saying goes. However, a slight revision in one's outer persona might help break through interview resistance, for instance. A facelift may brighten the surface of one's persona, but for a better, less costly change to one's personality, first consider improving communication skills. This non-invasive treatment will yield a greater return on one's investment, than an expensive facelift. Improving listening, questioning, clarification and techniques to elicit thoughtful feedback, will do more for one's "image" with a hiring manager than spending a lot of money on temporary fixes.

- **Profiling Personality on the Cheap**

If you do not have the time, resources, or interest in undertaking a full-blown battery of tests and inventories, there are other ways to profile your personality. There are shortcuts, which can work if not taken too seriously. Consider the following shortcut a starting point to creating your own profile. **First, review the section on Personality Types, and Holland's *Typology*. Second, select the descriptions that seem to fit your personality. Third, create a profile general enough to include other strengths of your personality.** The idea behind this exercise is to be comfortable with the notion that certain personalities fit better with certain jobs and work environments than others. Again, consider Holland's *Typology*. For instance, if you know that you are more comfortable in an organized, predictable environment, you already know enough to avoid startups, where job titles, communications and organizational structure are often vague and chaotic. On the other hand, if you have a high tolerance for ambiguity and chaos, a startup may be just your cup of tea.

Although more easily said than done, take time to look for hidden personality strengths and weaknesses, traits that may help or hinder occupational success.

Accentuating positive aspects of one's personality and subverting negative traits will empower the occupational journey. Knowing the weak links in your personality is akin to practicing the English proverb, "Forewarned is to be forearmed." For example, knowing that authoritative personalities strongly irritate you may help you think and react more strategically when being interviewed by this personality type. In this case, simply using better listening skills may do the trick.

☑ Personality: A Fascinating Subject

Personality is undeniably fascinating. If you are interested in more information on health and personality, I suggest you review several research citations provided by Pub Med, a service of U.S. National Institutes of Health Library of Medicine®. Pub Med provides free access to MEDLINE®, the NLM® database of indexed citations and abstracts.

Most of us have a basic idea of our "natural" interests and skills, but, when in doubt, consult with specialists in career development. Look to your local community college counseling centers, state employment agency, or licensed test specialists. They can be excellent resources of great assistance in helping anyone improve chances of long-term occupational success.

∫∆ Integrating Change

CHAPTER THREE

INTERESTS

The Energy behind Action

I was like a boy playing on the seashore, and diverting myself now and then finding a smoother pebble or a prettier shell than ordinary, whilst the great ocean of truth lay all undiscovered before me. [Isaac Newton]

Magnetic Attraction: Interests

Interests influence virtually every decision we make, from what we buy to where we travel, to who we marry, including those interests that affect our choice of work and careers. They are the work of our dreams and aspirations. They are, more scientifically, the emotional reaction to our physical and psychological environments. They are the feelings that cause us to focus on objects, events, and processes. More importantly, interests have the psychological power to draw one's attention to persons, places and things, which just about covers everything. To understand interests is to understand two important points: First, it does not matter where interests come from, whether they turn on like a light bulb, or are dropped from above by a stork into our consciousness. It is not where interests come from as much as what one does with them. Secondly, the sheer freedom to contemplate one's occupational interests is important because the freedom to choose allows us to control our occupational destinies. Nevertheless, freedom to choose means taking responsibility for one's occupational direction.

☑ The Laws of Interests

- **The Need to Explore**

Lawrence Siegel, industrial psychologist, and author of *Industrial Psychology*, would agree with Gardner Murphy's theory that we operate as biosocial creatures. Siegel concurs with Murphy that,

"*Interests are a product of the interaction of hereditary and environmental factors*" (pg. 127). Siegel and Murphy share the same model—**that interests are both cause and effect; that they arise out of one's interaction and integration with the physical and social environment**. This interaction has a profound influence on what we do, in our personal lives and our occupational lives. According to Lee Cronbach, professor, psychologist, and author of *Essentials of Psychological Testing*, **interests never become permanently fixed, but constantly reshape with more experience (p.419).** Interests change as our environment changes. I am forever impressed with those who find new and exciting ways to express their dreams, aspirations, and interests.

- **The Power to Attract**

Whether intrigued by an unsolved mystery, an exciting speaker, or a captivating article on the Internet, new interests can excite, inspire, motivate, and rouse one into action. Like Newton's concept of gravitation, interests have the power to pull one toward new and different directions, including new and different jobs and career paths.

Nevertheless, like two opposing forces, interests can attract attention in one direction and resist the same direction in another. *Have you ever been attracted to something new and exciting, only to hesitate because a little voice kept telling you to be cautious?* **Interests, by their very nature, cause emotional collisions between attraction and resistance, between intrigue and fear.** For a split second, or over a lifetime, these two opposing, emotional forces have the power to attract and resist, advance or impede, propel or retard one's personal development. How one handles these emotional dilemmas will determine, in large measure, one's occupational direction and success.

- **The Power to Set Direction**

Interests can stir the juices of imagination and move humans into action, on the big screen and on Main Street. Case in point. The affair between King Edward VIII and the beautiful Mrs. Wallis Simpson, a divorced, American socialite, was so strong that Edward abdicated the throne of England to marry Wallis.

Aside from romance, interests can range from scant to consuming, from fleeting to permanent, from casual to absolute, like the kind that sparked King Edward's love for Wallis. Interests result from interacting with people, places, and are recurrent themes, like those in a movie. One's interests can span from the simplest of hobbies to writing sensitive poetry, from volunteering at a local hospital to painting the Sistine Chapel. **Nevertheless, when it comes to interests, none is as important,**

or powerful, than those that affect work and careers. Interests, particularly new interests, can be as soft as a cool zephyr or abrupt as a Mack truck. They can pique attention or command the kind of attention that causes a jaw-dropping, 360-degree mid-career transformation. Occupational transformations can be dramatic, like the attorney who drops his or her partnership to dedicate his or herself to helping the poor.

☑ Work and Career Interests

Of the five behavioral dimensions, Interests is neglected most, but has the power to be one of the most influential when it comes to occupational choice. *Instead of one particular job or industry, what about looking at what motivates you most?* The glitz of a job can be alluring, for sure, but glitz is temporary. *Can you identify your motivators?* Skipping that question can be costly, especially to long-term job satisfaction. Nevertheless, one of the grand conundrums in job and career choice is choosing between the present or charging ahead into the future.

Real life and research has proven that interests play a dominant role in behavior, in general, but more specifically, in occupational choices. Ask a hundred people what interests them and most will easily rattle off a half dozen answers, from movies to collecting baseball cards. However, when it comes to the question about occupational choice, answers do not come as easily. That is because occupational choice rests more on what we wished we had done, than on what we are doing. I *wish* I had gone into architecture. I *wish* I had pursued medicine. I *wish* I had gone to college. And so on. In effect, unfulfilled interests and career aspirations sometimes linger over a lifetime, pushing for attention and resolution, smoldering as disappointments. These kinds of dilemmas force one to ask the age-old question of whether to stay put or change and follow one's dreams.

☑ Employment Innovation

It's not just organic LEDs, iPods, or GPS systems that catch our attention and cause us to open our pocket books. Consider the on-going advances in battery technology, solar technologies, and factory robotics and voice recognition innovations, not to mention proliferation of Internet cloud computing and social networking.

• Competition

To remain competitive, business has two main objectives. One is to refresh employee skills and knowledge, with up-to-date and training programs. The second is to create a new interest in the hearts and minds of their consumers, whether it is in soap or computers. Successful industries are constantly adjusting to competitive forces, decisions, and corporate interests. Healthcare and the military industrial complex, for example, will continue to undergo substantial change, compelled by political and international pressures to reduce costs and improve services.

- **Technological Improvements**

Every day the news covers stories about some high technology company facing another patent suit, over the incessant drive to be first to market. The stakes amount to gains and losses in the billions of dollars. Kodak, for example, the leader for decades in photographic film, was toppled by a new kind of film—silica—that has all but replaced the old standby, thirty-five millimeter film, now virtually gone, like the typewriter. To stretch the point a little further, consider that Apple Computer's balance sheet exceeds that of some US States. **Technological Improvements creates interests, opportunities, investments, occupations, wealth and, most importantly, jobs**.

- **Industrial Metamorphosis**

Renovation and reinvention is alive and well in today's world, businesses either change and remain competitive, or vanish into oblivion. Like a tsunami, changes hit business from all directions, including: competition, costs, regulations, capital replacement, and technological improvements. Businesses fight ever-increasing global competition, to say nothing of currency manipulation, intellectual property theft, knockoffs, and foreign subsidies. The drive to remain competitive creates new and interesting work and careers.

☑ Exploring Other Pastures

Other jobs and industries may occasionally pique our interests, like a moth to a flame. Whether out of need or simple curiosity, interests occasionally drift toward jobs and fields of business that are fascinating but unknown. Taking that leap of faith to use one's talents and acquire new skills to make a change will mean joining thousands of others in the labor market who are using secondary and post-secondary educational institutions to bridge the gap.

- **Interest Preference Tests**

Losing a sense of occupational interests can be unnerving, like being lost at sea. However, you can redirect the ship several different ways. You can use your wits and creativity, or you can chart a new direction using the latest horoscope. On the other hand, you can re-chart your career direction by taking educated clues by taking a few interest preference tests. They may take a little time, but they are painless and worth the exercise when administered by an experienced career counselor. Thousands of career-minded people have used career specialists to help them find their way to the occupational shore. Located at college counseling centers, private career counseling centers, and local state employment services, counselors can help unravel perplexing job interests. **Tests, such as the Holland Inventory, The Kuder Occupational Interest Survey, or the Strong Interest Inventory®, to name a few, can provide invaluable insights into new occupational directions. Just what one needs when self-direction is not working!**

- **Informational Meetings [the "Reverse" Interview]**

An informational interview is a great way to acquire insight into an occupation or industry that is of interest. The beauty of an informational meeting is that it comes equipped with trust and rapport. You do not have to create it. The relationship is between a "host-manager" and "guest-career explorer." Your goal, then, as the guest, is to learn as much as you can about the industry, company and departmental challenges faced by the manager. Informational meetings are important to those seeking to break into a new field. The process to securing an informational meeting takes several steps. Remember, the purpose of informational meetings is to receive guidance and advice. For managers, however, the payoff is recognition. Other important benefits to the manager include:

- Possibility of meeting a potential employee [there is always attrition and turnover].
- A genuine desire to offer sage advice about their industry and the means to a successful career

Step 1. Find an Interested Manager

First, find a manager willing to share his or her expertise. One of the best ways to obtain a face-to-face meeting with a manager is through a referral by a friend. They are good because employees have influence with managers, and managers have the authority to grant informational interviews. For a number of practical reasons, such as scheduled meetings, project commitments, or simply avoidance, convincing a manager to meet to discuss her or his industry with you can be an obstacle. In reality, however, most denials are soft. With a little persistence, many managers will grant an informational meeting.

Step 2. Asking to Meet for Advice and Counsel

Gather the courage to call a manager and introduce yourself with something like:

I am calling for professional advice. I am currently exploring other fields of employment and would like to ask your opinion and advise on how my background might fit into the xyz industry [add your own words].

If granted the meeting, express appreciation. Keep an open schedule, but be prepared to state a preference for date and time.

[Overcoming a Manager's Reluctance to Set Aside the Time]

However, if a manager does resist a request, be prepared to ask one or two short, open-ended questions. Let a manager offer as much information as he or she wishes. If his or her response is curt, and has tone of voice that is discouraging, consider asking for a referral to another manager. Now is the time to be more than a little pushy, but not irritating. It's a fine line. As a tradeoff for denying a request for an informational meeting, they may trade their denial by asking for a copy of your resume, a good will gesture, for sure, but who knows, maybe for a future job.

Step 3. The Informational Meeting

On the day of the meeting, greet the manager with something like:

Thanks for taking time to meet with me. As you know, I am exploring a career in your field, and would really appreciate your opinions and suggestions on how to proceed.

Plan for no more than 30-45 minutes, even though most informational meetings last an hour or so. Managers enjoy reaching into their memories for stories about their professional experience and success. In practice—who doesn't? **The manager ("teacher") answers questions and expresses opinions, whereas you, the "student," asks good questions, and listens carefully for references to the manager's challenges and stress points**. Over the course of a meeting, it should become clear how your personality, interests, and experience might fit the manager's notion of an ideal background. Your goal, remember, is to question the employer about problems and challenges, and the kinds of skills and experience that profile an ideal employee. Similar to opening a door to a closet filled with goodies, open-ended questions can quickly open the floodgates to great information. On the other hand, closed questions, those answered with a "yes," or "no" are great in a courtroom, but limiting during informational meetings. Using the following sample of open-ended questions can open the lines of communication to opinions, values, feelings, and information.

In what ways has your industry changed?

How has your company responded to . . . foreign competition . . . declining markets . . . being acquired?

In your opinion, what do you consider the ideal kind of background for this position?

Asking directed, open-ended questions is the best way to guide the line of inquiry toward specific questions and opinions on ideal qualifications. Make up your own questions, or use something like the following:

How has the nature of your work in your industry changed over the past several years?

What kinds of customers does your company serve?

How does your company stay competitive?

Who are your main competitors? Are there any in the local area?

What is the typical career path for those who work in your industry?

What kind of training is required to stay up with changes in your department?

What do you consider to be ideal qualifications and experience for those in your department?

What specific recommendations do you have for someone like me entering your industry?

(Listen carefully to this answer. How much overlap is there with your background?)

Step 4. Placing a Risky Bet: Switching Strategies

To a manager, informational sessions are fun because they are risk free. The benefits of providing information to a "student" include an opportunity to wander from subject to subject, issuing opinions, expressing conjectures, answering off the cuff, showing off a bit, even pontificating, free of any expectations, except to lend a helping hand to an aspiring career explorer. Whereas, "students" can ask any question or seek any opinion on how to succeed. When it comes to shifting the roles from student to applicant, watch out, the shift could be risky on several levels.

Because Informational meetings take advantage of built-in trust, and rapport—an expectation of an easy-going, friendly exchange between a teacher and a student—any change to that expectation could upset the apple cart. After all, the informational meeting was granted on the expectation of a "teacher-student" relationship. Switching intent risks loss of a manager's generosity. Think more about a swift, unceremonious, escort to the front door.

A Better Strategy

The better strategy is to listen and watch carefully for changes in managers' tone and demeanor. When the manager shifts from answering questions to asking more about your interests and experience, this may be the sign that you may be less than a student and more like an applicant.

Step 5. Taking Initiative to Close the Meeting

After 45 minutes or so, take the initiative to conclude the meeting, unless you sense they are switching their focus your way. Express appreciation for time taken to meet with you. Most managers will appreciate your sensitivity to their schedule. Initiate closure with something like:

Thanks for taking time out of your busy schedule to meet with me. I thoroughly enjoyed our meeting. You have given me a good deal of insight into your industry and the qualities it takes to succeed. If you know of other people you think may help me in my career search, I would be extremely grateful for any referrals.

Taking the initiative to end a meeting signals a couple of things: one, it shows that you can manage time, and two, controlling conclusions conveys sensitivity to your host's schedule, engendering appreciation and emotional, if not practical, reciprocity

☑ Finding Your Interests Online

It may seem too obvious, but searching online job postings may lead to interesting job and career paths. **Online postings are a good reflection of an ever-changing array of potential jobs and career paths.** In spite of the technical jargon, job postings are fascinating because they reflect the job needs of virtually every major industry and company in the United States. If you are looking for inspiration from interesting job postings, this is the place to look.

Search companies that are transforming themselves. Take the word of experts and employment professionals (like me): companies are in constant change, continually creating interesting, challenging opportunities. Your challenge, therefore, is to search for job and career opportunities that complement your personality, interests, and experience.

If your occupational commitments have left you feeling shortchanged, you may need to expand your range of career interests. You can blame bad choices, but misplaced priorities are also partly to blame. A combination of too few interests and misplaced priorities can make a career seeker out of step with the labor market. Like the physician who listens and probes with good questions for signs of poor health, you may need to do the same with a career path that has skipped a few beats. *Are your interests in line with your skills and talents? Are you resisting changes to your job search strategies?*

$\int \Delta$ *Integrating Change*

CHAPTER FOUR
EXPERIENCE

Bodies in Motion

**Skill is the unified force of experience, intellect, and passion in their operation. [John Ruskin].
Few people even scratch the surface; much less exhaust the contemplation of their own
experience.** [Randolph Bourne]

Experience

As an individual strength, experience, more specifically employment experience, is a key bargaining
chip when it comes to occupational strategies. How we play the experience card can make all the
difference to occupational success. **How experience is described in resumes and explained during
an interview determines its strength**. Although an integral measure of occupational progress,
work experience often goes unnoticed until one confronts an unexpected change in employment. It
is at this point that the importance of experience becomes obvious. Used in a resume or cited during
an interview, experience history is the most tangible means to occupational success.

Unlike personality, work history is pliable, expandable, like a bank account, where one can continually
add valuable skills and knowledge, in order to enrich one's wealth of experience.

Our view of the world of work and our ability to master it depends a great deal on one's experience.
Although a challenge to stay up with the ever-changing world of work, the opportunities created
each day are breathtaking. However, engaging in the process will require an assessment of your
current wealth of experience and decisions made on the best way to invest it to create occupational
success.

☑ Qualifications on Display

Most employers want to see results and contributions. They want to know applicants have solved problems, how processes were improved, how interdepartmental communications were increased, why one method improved efficiencies when others did not. They want to know the how, the why, and the when. Therefore, revisiting one's work experience, using a different set of filters, will have its benefits. Taking a fresh look at your experience in the context of today's work world may inspire insight into new plans and strategies. Taking a step back to get a fresh look at experience, through the filters of your personality and your short and long-term interests can mean the difference between an old, stale resume, for example, and a fresh, compelling story of growth and success. Adding acquired skills, forgotten contributions, or new responsibilities, can brighten an otherwise drab work history. Re-examining the past, in the context of today's challenges and your strengths will help you recall, organize, and reprioritize your work experience.

- **Individual Strengths**

In the scheme of things, it is easy to forget the difference our experience has made in the success of our employers. Condensing important experience into thought-sized "grabbers" is a challenge. However, if you want to upgrade, uplift, strengthen, or create a more accurate portrait of yourself, then concentrate on emphasizing your strongest strengths, skills and talents. Although there are, many ways to improve one's experience image, you may want to consider the following question: *Given your work experience, what skills and talents are unique to you? Are some work skills and talents easier for you compared to others?* For instance, are you completely at ease leading a group discussion? Are you confident in making group presentations? Does the notion of "stage fright" mean nothing to you? If so, consider yourself one of a few with a special sense of confidence. Have you a memory that impresses others at work? Could your memory be one of your strong suits? Is your communication with others so good that you could, as one client put it, "talk to a stump?" If so, jobs requiring strong communication skills may be right up your alley. Nevertheless, review your experience for special talents that stand out from others.

- **Skills and Talents**

As the precursor to experience and careers, skills come in all shapes, sizes, and descriptions. Skills run the gamut, from solving the Rubik Cube to eye-hand coordination, or from computer programming to commercial design. Whether learned or natural, most talents develop over time, further honed by knowledge and practice. Over time, experience clusters toward technical and interpersonal skills.

Over time, one's skills and talents gradually merge into general problem-solving abilities. These abilities are further organized and strengthened with training, education, and practice.

- **Specialized Knowledge**

In today's world, technical experience includes information applications and systems such as: database programming, spreadsheet applications, and word processing. One look at the help wanted ad in today's newspaper and online tells the story. It is almost overwhelming how business has come to rely on information technology.

- **Work Contributions**

In many ways, work contributions provide the bedrock to one's employment history. Because of the importance of work history, you would think work contributions would be easy to write, but you would be mistaken. Writing job contributions that sound compelling is difficult. Why? Because most of us have little idea, what impact our work has had on any measure of job success. However, in spite of this deficiency, it is still important to try to create a work history that references your unique contributions.

- **Communications Proficiency**

Our world is increasingly dependent on computer and social networking for communications. Therefore, most managers will probe your knowledge and experience with common office computer applications, such as email, word processing, document management, spreadsheet, and Internet usage.

Another form of communications is your interpersonal skills. This skill is a gauge of potential teamwork interactions. How you have interacted with others, particularly supervisors, points to future success in dealing with others, including potential colleagues and leaders. From my experience, managers know that getting "along with the boss" is basic to an applicant's future success in the work place. Nothing is worse for managers than having tension with one of their employees. However, managers also know that applicants and employees are not perfect. **Seasoned managers know, for example, that signs of strong, positive interpersonal communications will often compensate for minor deficiencies in experience and expertise.** Not to diminish its importance, but occasionally, hiring managers will focus on written communication skills.

☑ Convergence of Work Experience

Most of us have an idea about how to define a job, but how many can define the concept of a career? I see careers as a single strand or string of related jobs. Experts in the field define "career" in more detail. Herr, Cramer, Pope, (2009) and Davis (1871-1955), **define career as, "*the total constellation of psychological, sociological, educational, physical, economic, and chance factors that combined to influence the nature and significance of work in the total lifespan of any given individual"*** (pg.7). In a position paper, Davis concluded that the concept of careers included, ". . . *a person's creation of career patterns, decision-making style, integration of life roles, values expression, and life-role self-concepts*" (pg.2). I still like the string analogy.

- **The DNA of Careers**

It is hard to think of work and experience without contemplating what constitutes a career. You might think about a large ball of string, strands of cotton, collected day-by-day, overlapping, lacing, and skill over skill, gaining size and form. Like overlapping strands of string, most careers grow out of a series of jobs, some short in duration, others over a lifetime, connected by common skills and expertise. Like individual DNA, our skills, personality traits, aptitudes, principles, values, and interests, constantly interconnect and reinforce one another. We may change jobs and careers, but we continue to carry with us our physical and psychological DNA. Perseverance, problem solving, and fairness and honesty, along with other basic values like them, are imbedded in our being, like eye color, carried from one work setting to another. For example, an emotionally satisfying internship in accounting, for a community non-profit agency, could easily lead to a career at a worldwide, non-profit foundation. Likewise, A Regional Occupational Program (ROP) class in carpentry could lead one with new self-confidence to a career in the solar industry. Foundation skills, talents, principles, and values can serve to thread together work, experience, and careers.

☑ Occupational Dissonance

Occupational dissonance can be nasty. It can force one to change occupational direction, abruptly and without warning. Whether, real or rumored layoffs, outsourced jobs, unwarranted or unexpected transfers, or, worst of all, vague criticisms from supervision, occupational dissonance is a universally difficult state of mind. Changes in business conditions, such as a change in supervision, low sales, stronger competitors, can also create a sense of employment dissonance, which adversely affect security and predictability, self-esteem and optimism. Nevertheless, one can turn negative changes into positive motivators. On the other hand, turning occupational dissonance into positive action involves personal change.

☑ Building on Change

We integrate experience in response to changes in our environment. We react, instinctively, to a moving car, an uneven sidewalk, or an emotional event. We seek pleasant experiences and avoid unpleasant ones, as any biosocial being would. How we integrate or react to change—good, bad, or neutral—makes up the sum total of our experience. In effect, we first react to our physical and social worlds before moving with or against our reactions. Whether you simply contemplate change or experience change first hand, or feel pulled by serendipity, random opportunity, or by conscious decision, successful change will depend on a number of actions, including how well you plan an occupational course of action.

☑ Taking Experience to the Next Level

Careers often begin to mature within the first three-to-five years of work. Basic skills acquired in high school or college quickly develop under guidance, training, and close supervision. During the early, formative years of one's career, workers frequently migrate from one job to another, developing new skills and talents. These early bird employees are prime in the eyes of other employers who lure away new workers with better pay and opportunities. Migrating from one company or industry to another is like salmon looking for better spawning grounds. **Migrating to other employers often leads to better pay, more challenges, more responsibilities, and increased opportunities for growth, challenge and development.**

Job change is one way to satisfy dreams of greater occupational and career fulfillment. Like the annual migration of swallows to the Southern California Mission of San Juan Capistrano, the pursuit of better work and jobs is natural, almost instinctual. Most early jobs have little in common, except for income or a manager's promise of better things to come. Therefore, workers often move to other jobs where they can trade their newly acquired skills and talents for better opportunities.

- **Transferrable Experience**

Skills considered transferrable are able to compensate for differences between jobs and occupations. For example, leadership skills, qualities of former military officers, can compensate for lack of specific job experience. A newly hired executive may not need to know a lot about their new employer's product lines. Instead, what the new employer wants is the executive's management skills.

How does one know what skills are transferrable to a new job or industry? The most direct way is to compare your skills and talents with the job or industry of interest. The process may take research, and an informational interview or two, but the results may tell if you are a good match or not. If one is lucky, sometimes, a manager will be more interested in an applicant's transferrable skills rather their specific job skills. When an interviewer remarks something like, "*Oh, don't worry, we will train you,*" you can be sure they see your transferrable skills as potentially useful. Who knows? Your communications style, spreadsheet aptitude, or your sense of optimism may compensate for lack of specific experience. Therefore, before you start a job search, identify your transferrable skills as they may prove very useful in bridging the skills gap.

- **Transferrable Qualifications**

The following table includes a sampling of transferrable qualifications, such as leadership. Broad skill groupings like "leadership" and "communications," serve as umbrellas for related skills that are also transferrable across jobs, companies, and occupations. Assigning responsibilities or recommending solutions reflects "leadership" in the minds of the readers. **How many different kinds of jobs can you think of that require some level of leadership experience?** If looked at closely, I think you will see that most jobs require some level of leadership.

Leadership	Communications	Research
Administrating	Addressing	Collecting
Supervising	Writing	Analyzing
Assigning	Arbitrating	Diagnosing
Recommending	Recommending	Evaluating

Analysis	Quantitative	Creativity
Inventing	Auditing	Establishing
Examining	Analyzing	Initiating
Evaluating	Budgeting	Instituting
Calculating	Calculating	Inventing

Teaching	Aiding/Caring	Administrative
Advising	Assisting	Arranging
Instructing	Clarifying	Cataloguing
Coaching	Coaching	Classifying
Communicating	Counseling	Compiling

☑ **Reengineering Experience**

Even the thought of having to reengineer one's skills or experience can cause a grimace. Just the thought of more education and training can throw a person off balance and test one's sense of self-self-confidence. On the other hand, realizing that one may be out of step in today's world of work may a wakeup call to action. Reality does have its benefits, something like a flu shot.

• **Personal Reinvention**

Although job and career transformations often result in wonderful outcomes, most transformations require a fair dose of hard work along with copious amounts of perseverance. Career transformations result from an infinite number of sources, but two sources account for most. The first comes from being compelled to find new occupational interests. The second comes from simply admiring another's success.

Transferring a Background in Defense Electronics to Healthcare Manufacturing

An electronics technician in the defense industry knew he had to make an occupational change. Not that he wanted to change jobs, but large defense contracts were ending and he felt anxious about the future. However, he felt confident that he could transfer his experience, he just did not know where. His first step was research. He explored roughly, thirty or so industries, before coming across healthcare. He admitted he had scant information about the industry, and no direct experience, but saw a possible fit. Next, he continued his research into the industry and uncovered several trade publications at his local library, which led to several Internet sites where he found a number of references on "healthcare manufacturing systems." With that, he identified several healthcare manufactures involved in test and measurement applications and compiled a list of company names and contact numbers. With a better understanding of how his background might transfer, he secured a courtesy informational meeting with a healthcare manufacturing manager. Coupled with advice and guidance, he began to feel more confident about transferring his electronic test skills to medical device manufacturing. Given a referral to a nearby medical device company, he then made contact with their manufacturing manager who gave him a lot of good advice and a schedule to several trade shows. He attended one show and made several more contacts. They, in turn, provided several face-to-face interviews and two job offers, one local, one out of area. A lot of work? Yes. Many steps? Yes. Luck? Yes. Transformation is not easy. It can take six or more months, but results may be worth a lifetime of occupational success.

Reengineering a career in engineering into private Entrepreneurship

An experienced, quality control engineer, secure in his job, well paid, and appreciated by his manager, but nonetheless, felt uneasy about his career direction. He felt stifled by restrictive oversight, rigid delivery schedules, and squeezed by a tight, corporate philosophy. He felt motivated to change. We explored his interests, hobbies, and activities outside of work. He said he admired his friend who worked as an independent contractor. He saw his friend as having a quality of work life that was appealing—that it appeared to give him the freedom to create his own success. I suggested he take a day to ride along with his friend on service calls to see first-hand how he managed a typical day's work. A couple of weeks later, my client reported the experience eye opening, a transformative experience. He negotiated a training position with his friend, who recognized my client's appreciation for quality control and hard work. I heard through the grapevine that he started his own company, that spirit of entrepreneurship drove him to uncover another way of managing his aspirations.

- **An Occupational Tune-up**

How much of your personal and occupational strengths you have forgotten or neglected? At the very least, even a minor tune-up of skills and knowledge will increase self-confidence and assurance, to say nothing of one's improved sense of optimism. **Why not improve your skills? Why not reengineer your strengths and talents? Even if you're not sharpening your technical skills,**

why not reshape your attitude and outlook? If *Behavioral Strengths and Employment Strategies* adds to your knowledge or optimism, or prompts a self-examination, isn't that a good thing?

☑ Integrating Experience in Motion ∫Δ

The concept, "Integrating Experience," is worth remembering, as it is the thesis of this book. Experience is the result of Integrating Change. Therefore, change is an integral part of our existence, our paths to success or failure, occupational or otherwise. Nevertheless, one way to describe the concept of experience is to use two mathematical symbols, ∫ and **Δ,** which are often used in Calculus. Imagine them representing the process of Integrating Change, thereby acquiring experience. The First symbol, the integral, ∫, represents the process of integrating one's reactions to internal and external events. The second mathematical symbol, the delta, **Δ**, represents internal and external physical and psychological events, ranging from a simplest, superficial scratch to our deepest emotional reaction to grief or joy. Combined, the two symbols, ∫ and **Δ**, symbolize the process of

Integrating Change, the process of living, the process of growth and development. **Moreover, how we integrate change becomes the crux of our experience and our success in the world of work.** Note, I use the expression; ∫∆ Integrating Change, at the end of each chapter to remind us of its importance.

∫∆ *Integrating Change*

CHAPTER FIVE
RESILIENCE

Resilience: A Perfect Defense

Resilience can be described as a behavioral strength, the strength to withstand, cope with, or recover from adverse situations, the kind often encountered during a job search. More specifically, resilience is an emotionally protective mechanism, one of five behavioral strengths cited in this book as important to long-term job and career success. Therefore, it is not unusual that resiliency and self-affirmation overlap to provide maximum protection for the job seeker.

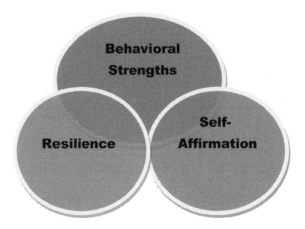

Thus, the thesis of this book is that we integrate job and career development through three dimensions:

(1) the Behavioral, which includes Resilience and Self-Affirmation; (2) the Strategic, which includes research and interviewing, and (3) the contextual dimension of the career actualization process. As a behavioral strength, resilience overlaps with the attributes found in self-affirmation. Psychological mechanisms such as resilience and self-affirmation can be inferred from tests, but for most of us resilience one of those behavioral strengths we feel well before we experience actual adversity.

☑ Behavioral Strength No.5

Resilience is a blend of positive behavioral strengths, including one's sense of inner self-affirmation, and optimism about future employment. Resilience is one of those vague emotions that can be inferred to exist, but not observed. Combined with self-affirmation, resilience helps us cope with the adversity felt during a job search, when much of the interaction with employers is demoralizing. Resilience helps us bounce back from setbacks and adversities, thereby helping us maintain our sense of self-worth and esteem. Resilience helps us accept the world as it comes our way, whereas our inner self-affirmation validates our on-going sense of self-worth. Resilience and self-affirmation "work" to protect us in spite a failed interview, or a sharp rejection from an employer, by serving as important behavioral defense mechanisms. *Most of us use both protective mechanisms to varying degrees.* In their paper, *The Psychology of Change: Self-Affirmation and Social Psychological Intervention*, Geoffrey L. Cohen1 and David K. Sherman, surveyed other researchers who likewise, were able to isolate coping skills where resilience and self-affirmation combined to reinforce one another.

Research (Tesser, A., Martin, L. L., & Cornell, D. P., 1996) has shown that a sense of personal affirmation reinforces resilience when we are confronted with negative feedback, criticisms, and threats to self-image...

☑ Coping with Adversity

- **Self-affirmation**

Numerous studies confirm self-affirmation theory *(Cohen, Aronson, & Steele, 2000; Correll, Spencer, & Zanna, 2004; Liu & Steele, 1986; Tesser & Cornell, 1991; Steele, C. M. (1988).* **Research show self-affirmation reduces defensive reactions in stressful situations, as well as threats to personal values, such as a belief in fairness** *(Sherman & Cohen, 2002, 2006).* Other studies have found that asserting affirmations, such as belief in helping one's neighbor, will reduce sensitivity and aggressive reactions to threats and criticism from others, another form of resilience.

According to *Gilbert, Pinel, Wilson, Blumberg, & Wheatley (1998),* **behavioral strengths, such as resilience and self-affirmation, combine to protect us against emotional threats,** such as an impending job interview or the fear of being rejected by a screening panel of peers. On the other hand, studies have found that self-affirmation, such as believing ourselves to be honest or empathetic, increase trust and a sense of openness, thereby reducing the likelihood of defensive reactions to stress questions, the kind asked during a job interviews

In a sociological study of men, women and children from the Great Depression era, G.H. Elder identified an *"adaptive, competent self"* (p. 249), a sense of *"personal worth … inner security" (pp… 11 247, 249)*, *"an active coping orientation to the environment,"* a *"capacity for sustaining effort and relationships, even in the face of obstacles,"* *"flexibility in the ability to learn and grow from mistakes,"* *"the resilience to rise above setbacks,"* and a faith in ability to adapt adequately to changing circumstances* (p. 247).

Consciously or unconsciously, we use a variety of coping strengths and skills to reduce the stress encountered during periods of emotional stress, such as those we often encounter during a job search. Known to psychologists and other specialists as *defense mechanisms*, we use simple, practical coping strategies, to sophisticated self-affirmations to reduce the sting from disappointing events. Whatever coping mechanism you use, such as reaffirming your core values, take some time to assess their use in your pursuit of that next job or career change.

- **Core Values**

Those who affirm core values, such as honesty and fairness, are more likely to recognize similar feelings in others. *Affirming core values reduces defensive reactions to threatening situations, such as interviews*. On a practical level, having a good sense of your basic values, from work commitment to generosity will help you feel less defensive during a tough interview, for example. Less defensiveness will generally result in better rapport, greater self-confidence, and more control over negative emotions, such as pessimism, which can undermine one's self-image and worth.

- **Self-Image and Self-worth**

We continually add bits and pieces of (hopefully) positive feedback into our self-image, we protect with resilience. What we hear and see from others, is what we largely project to others. It is what others see in us, what others might recognize as that "sweetheart of a person," or that "friendly, level-headed teacher" or that "super salesman." Our self-worth, for example, can guard against the effects of a negative interview, or a stinging job rejection. As a coping mechanism, resilience is a powerful behavioral strength. The same goes for Self-esteem.

- **Self-confidence**

The sting of losing a job is universal. It makes little difference whether management consolidates, outsources, or eliminates jobs; virtually all employees will do what they can to protect their self-worth and confidence. According to *C.M. Steel (1988)*, self-worth and integrity make up feelings and core values that affirm that we are, "*competent, good, coherent, autonomous, stable, capable of free choice and of controlling important outcomes*" (pg. 262). For instance, under the intense pressure from a confrontation, most of us will preserve our self-confidence. *Tesser, A., & Cornell, D. P. (1991)* found that those who use self-affirmation to deal with threats, such as strong criticisms or impending failures, do so without persistent or marked anxiety. According to *Cohen, Aronson, Steel (2000)*, self-affirmations provide emotional protection from adverse situations by increasing acceptance of more risk and less defensive reactions.

☑ Finding Success in the Employer's Domain

The path to successful employment requires the use of the five personal behavioral strengths and five smart employment strategies, the kind of strategies that facilitate interactions with employers. More specifically, success in the employer's domain or the labor market will require the use specific employment strategies, beginning with action and perseverance, research skills into employment interests, along with interview and negotiating skills. Success in the employer domain will require best use of your behavioral strengths and employment strategies, strategies outlined in the next five chapters of this book.

☑ Resilience: protection against rejection

Resilience protects our self-esteem from threatening situations, by helping us react and integrate adverse events. When tested, we pull from our reservoir of protective mechanisms ways that counteract negative experiences and increase our self-confidence. Similarly, searching for Jobs and careers is an on-going exercise in building resilience to adversity. Some have said that the road to success is paved with disappointment and heartbreak, but, let me assure you, the road gets smoother as you go.

The next five chapters cover the five practical employment strategies critical to successfully managing the challenges of a job or career change.

∫Δ Integrating Change

CHAPTER SIX
ACTION

Converting Vision into Action

If wishes were horses, beggars would ride. [16th-Century proverb and rhyme suggests it is useless to wish. Results are better achieved through action].

Successful people keep moving. They make mistakes, but they don't quit. [Conrad Hilton].

Action Precedes Success

The pursuit of happiness is the chase of a lifetime. Achieving success or happiness starts with action, contemplated or actual. As a basic strategy to achieving occupational success, the idea of action can cover a lot of ground. It can begin, like a runner off the starting block, with a simple desire or the motivation to get started. I am not talking about the kind of motivation that takes you to the store for milk or the kind that makes you grab the popcorn during half time. **The kind of action I am referring to is the kind that which comes from losing a job, or feeling a sense of distress, anxiety, and gloom.**

Positive events are easy to deal with. It is the negative ones make a person twist and turn. Nevertheless, dealing with negative events is what drives us forward toward change, growth, more insight, and a sense of renewed optimism. More specifically, if you are one of those experiencing adversity, what actions are you planning to take? *What will you do next*? You can take many steps forward, but unless you lay out a plan to handle the journey, success may be an uphill battle. Accepting the notion that action begins with a sense of optimism is important because without a positive view to the future, one is likely to sit out the game. However, simply accepting the notion that optimism creates action does not lead directly to success. Not yet! You may have opened an important gateway to success, but to get to the other side will require more effort. Your first action, then, is to write your plan. The plan does not have to be fancy. A simple draft will do. With regular revisions, you can turn a draft plan into a nicely contoured roadmap to occupational success.

☑ Action #1. The How to Plan

"If you don't know where you're going, you might end up some place else." (Yogi Berra). Based on my consulting experience, most job seekers strike out on their journey without any semblance of a real plan. Most plan as they go, thinking they are following a plan. If your plan is to wing it, as you go be prepared to be buffeted by the winds of change. Even the simplest of plans, like a short grocery list, will serve as a starting point. Jot down a few important ideas, followed by a question mark. Start the list with a combination of: relocation, library, contacts, resume, interview attire, potential employers, classes, or friends and colleagues. Some you can answer with a simple yes or no, like, relocation. Others, such as how your plan will affect those closest to you or what means most to you in your next job will take more thought. **Questions, answers, and key ideas will provide a sense of direction to your plan.** Resist the urge to sidestep the process. Blasting off resumes, willy-nilly, before sighting your target is the perfect definition of chaos. Hold off any kind of shotgun approach until you can clearly see what, to whom, where, and how to target your efforts.

How and when you plan your search is up to you. You can make it comprehensive, with graphs and diagrams, or modest, drafted on the backside of an envelope. Consider your plan anything you wish: a map, a path, a blueprint, a diagram. It may be nothing more than scribbled, handwritten notes on the backside of a grocery list. **Start with an Internet search or visit to the library to research job search strategies.** Nevertheless, beware of procrastination, that nasty bug can sideline the best of plans. Immunize yourself against procrastination. Decide to start your planning as soon as possible, with a hard and fast start date, even if you do nothing more than write down a simple one sentence outline, based on this book's five strategies. In other words, checkmark your research, resume, interviewing, and negotiation. **Commit yourself to taking action. Any action, but start**.

- **Planning Use of Your Employment Strategies**

Strategies are free for the taking. However, like fruit at the farmer's market, most are tasty, but not all are ripe. Some strategies are worth pursuing and others are not worth the paper they are written on. Nevertheless, like a good shopper, make sure your basket contains the best ones. One bad apple or strategy, like scattering resumes everywhere, can easy contaminate a sense of optimism. Approach your choice of strategies carefully, so as not to waste precious time and resources.

Not only are strategies free, they can vary, from a to z, from newspaper postings to corporate websites, from radio and TV, to social networking, from Internet Job boards to highway billboards, from industry web publications to workshop networking, from cold calling to informational interviews. **Any strategy that results in progress is worthwhile, but the most effective, in my experience, includes employee referrals, social networking, and informational interviews.** You might consider the local State Department of Employment your best strategy, or cold calling. However, virtually every strategy relies on some planning. Therefore, before you put any strategy into action, be sure to connect them to your plan.

Personal and occupational success depends on a host of factors, many within your control, and many more out of your control. Too little planning and off the cliff you go. Nevertheless, too much planning may result in paralysis by analysis.

- **Conserve Energy, Time, and Financial Resources**

Most job searches are nonlinear, that is, they start and stop, hit difficulties, are sporadic, leap forward and fall backward, and occasionally fall flat. **To sidestep disaster, choose strategies that tap your communication style and strengths.** If you are very good over the phone, concentrate some of your efforts on cold calling. If you write a mean report and tight, concise correspondence, concentrate on written communication. Connect your strategies to your strengths and interests.

There are no perfect strategies. No two people take similar employment paths. We are all different; therefore our strengths and strategies are different. Some of us are better at planning, whereas others of us are better at marketing. My advice: be reasonably balanced and use several proven strategies, such as polishing your resume, or honing your Internet search skills, or actively participating in local transition groups.

- **Attention on Your Job Market**

Start your search of occupational trends with local, regional, and national industries, trade and professional associations, and state or local governments. Search for annual disclosure reports, such as a public SEC 10-K Report, which summarizes company activities, such as acquisitions, executive compensation, stock options, lawsuits, and other significant issues of potential interest to stock holders and job seekers. These kinds of directories contain vast amount of information, but do not include jobs openings. For those, you have to visit a company's website, which typically links to their career site.

- **Periodic Measurements**

Almost as soon as you go into action, testing your choice of strategies begins. "Testing" begins with positive or negative reviews of your resume, for example, and from informal, face-to-face meetings with others.

- **Shift Directions**

Similar to a good stock fund, diversifying strategies is smart. If one strategy is not working, such as relying on newspaper job ads, shift to another strategy. Experience, experimentation, advice, and feedback from others, will regulate and improve your strategies. Before committing too much energy, take preemptive steps to offload strategies that do not appear to be working. For example, your opinions of employers can change, on a dime. That employer you thought so little of yesterday, today is terrific, according to a new friend you met in a network group. **Continually revise or toss out bad strategies and out-of-date or inaccurate information.** Stay open to change. Adapt by taking small or large steps. How you shift strategies is up to you. From a practical perspective, competing for employment in today's world works—if you accept the notion that good things can come out of adversity; that competition provides opportunities to reaffirm and improve your coping and communication skills, which is useful not only determining your occupational success, but in all aspects of life.

- **Room for Assistance**

There are as many ways to approach a plan, but they all include guidance. **However, for a low cost, fast review of an alternative plans, you might want to search the Internet for, "career transition."** If the information and links you find are too overwhelming, you might want to consult a career counselor. They are available at most community colleges or universities. Check their websites for references to counseling services. Most services are at nominal or no cost and the results may be just the spark you need to get things on track. Consider as many options as you can and then select those that best fit in your comfort zone.

☑ Action #2. Provisions

Preparation for action starts with provisions—not food or drink, but more on the level of communication tools, such as computers and printers, telephones and software programs. Such provisions serve as a job seeker's lifeline to the world of work.

- **Electronic Communications**

Today's computer is what the pencil was to the past. Today, a computer is an absolute necessity. It is almost impossible to conduct any kind of job search without a computer. If you do not have a computer, your library does. Although you can get by without a printer, before you do, consider their capabilities: most are wireless, most can fax and most can scan. Finally, when it comes to the telephone, think about mobility around the clock. Be sure to create an outgoing message that is clear, professional, and upbeat. Employers will judge you by what they hear.

- **Internet Access**

Considerer Internet access of prime importance. You can do without most other tools in your arsenal of job search strategies, including not having a resume, but for sheer access to employers, the Internet is indispensable. It is hard to find a more cost effective means of communicating with others. Besides voice, what was new and unique in the past is now commonplace. Commercial programs from Skype.com or Cisco.com, for example, offer video and voice communications, thereby cutting employment costs for both the applicant and the employer by eliminating travel for the initial interview.

- **Your Resume**

It may not be obvious, but resumes reflect the writer's personality, interests, and experience. Consider your resume your campaign flyer. Chapter Eight covers the subject of resumes in detail. Suffice it to say, that your resume should reflect your three essential strengths, your personality, your interests, and your experience. Consider them the big three.

- **Employment References**

Virtually all company application forms require several references. Comply with the employer's request, but append a note above or below the reference section with the following: "*Please do not contact any of my employment references without my permission. Thank you.*"

- **Binders, Folders, Contact Logs, Notebooks, and Calendars**

Resources like notebooks and calendars are indispensible. Create your own system or use someone else's, in order to collect and log important information, including: calls received and/or made, or to make, schedules, visits, plans, or notes. Also, keep track of emails, telephone numbers, and correspondence.

It may seem obvious, but organizing information by job, project, and topic, or by company, will help your mission. You may want to sort job ads and Internet postings by industry, location, or job type. Make a list of friends, colleagues, business associates, college alumni, and professional societies. Sort companies by location, telephone, email, website, and contact name. Take your pick. It is your system to devise. Try an Excel spreadsheet. Develop a calendar for appointments. Whatever works best. If stored electronically, make sure to back up your information.

- **Draft Correspondence**

Prepare several generic cover letters, email messages, and a mock job application. Creating individualized correspondence and filling out numerous employment applicants will be made much easier.

- **Attire**

Generally," business casual attire" is acceptable for a job interview. However, attire is often in the eye of the beholder. For that reason, you may want to visit chapter Nine, Interviews, for some tips on the topic of interview attire. However, as has been noted, of all the things related to appearance, one's smile is the most important.

☑ Action #3. Marketing

Start your marketing campaign by organizing your resources into a coherent program. You can sit back and wait for inquiries to roll in, but passive marketing will likely fail to produce meaningful results. Instead, decide to approach your campaign by taking active, assertive strategies to market your capabilities.

- **Self-directed Marketing**

Taking your campaign to employers requires strategies that involve communication and marketing acumen. Promotional skills, natural for some of us, but learned by most, include the ability to influence others. Convincing others to accept our experience, for example, during an interview, is pure self-promotion. Many profess they have little or no sales and promotional skills, but the fact is, we all have some. Have you ever convinced someone to accept your advice? Have you ever influenced or convinced others to take a position similar or different from yours or their own? Convincing others to accept your ideas or opinions requires the ability to sell yourself and your ideas. I strongly suspect you have the capability to sell yourself, but just need to brush up on your self-promotional skills

- **Your Message**

Now, you will need to develop strategies to market your "message." You want others to know how terrific you are (personality), how focused you remain (interests), and most importantly, how relevant your work (experience) is to their operations. Don't hold back. Tell the world of work that you have arrived. Don't be shy about marketing yourself. We see and feel effects of marketing every day, every waking hour. It is the backbone of our consumer economy. Marketing is all around us, in stores, on billboards, on and in buses, on streets, in blogs, tweets, YouTube, and social networks. It all seems natural and effortless, so your self-marketing is an acceptable part of success in the grand scheme of things. Then again, do not overdo it. Like the scales of justice, there is a delicate balance between blasting a message, boom box style, willy-nilly, and a directed, well thought out marketing campaign. You be the judge, but also solicit others' opinions.

Putting skills, talents, and energy into a job campaign requires several hats: campaign manager, marketing manager, and finance manager. You are like the small business owner who answers every telephone call, handles every complaint, and is responsible for every success and failure. You are the master of your own self-promotion campaign. You are your campaign.

- **A PERT Approach**

Too much responsibility? Too overwhelming? One suggestion is to break the plan into manageable, bite-sized tasks. If need be, at first, take small, easy steps. Create your own modified PERT chart (Project Evaluation Review Technique), by listing tasks to complete on the left side of a page, and the time-to-complete dates across the upper edge of the page. Use your PERT chart to organize tasks by importance, for example, by "date to complete." **The beauty of a PERT is that it can highlight progress**.

- **Revisions to Your Campaign**

Marketing plans are never perfect. Remember, most job searches create their own "soup" of emotions, and questions. Gleeful prospects of a new adventure are mixed with doubt and uncertainty, and then reality sets in. Questions, practical and serious crash our consciousness. *What do I wear to an interview? How do make contacts and get referrals? What should I say in my correspondence? Do I need to relocate? To whom do I turn? How do I make my house payments?* As hard as it may be, resist asking yourself a flood of questions until you have first drafted your plan.

- **Active Marketing is Tough Work**

Active marketing is tough work. Ask anyone who has gone through a major job transition how difficult it is. Cold calling, networking with strangers, and engaging with transition groups can test a person's ability to communicate with different people. Uncomfortable and awkward as it may be at first, active marketing, will improve with practice, and with trial and error. Making mistakes, suffering errors, and enduring failed strategies, although agonizing at times, will shorten the time it takes to reach one's goals. Communication, for example, will steadily improve, becoming more fluid, precise, organized, and professional sounding. To get your marketing campaign off the ground, off the page, and into the hands of employers, your next step will be to start promoting yourself.

Whatever plan or method you chose, continue to modify and adjust it as you go. Just remember, nothing is perfect. However, while you are at it, toss procrastination in the trashcan, or put it on the shelf, away from your consciousness. There will be plenty of time to procrastinate later.

☑ **Resisting Action**

One of the toughest challenges any of us has to face is managing unpleasant occupational change, particularly those associated with employment. **However, in my experience, negatives often result in positive occupational change, in different ways, but better.**

- **Homeostasis**

Unlike emotions, homeostasis operates as an inherent, biologic mechanism to maintain one's physiological balance. Homeostasis resets, so to speak, our physiologic system to normal, regulating, for example, blood pressure and heartbeat. **On another level, homeostasis can operate against our moving us out of our comfort zone, even to the extent of changing to achieve positives,**

including better occupational strategies and success. George Leonard, author of *Mastery*, reports that homeostasis can operate to prevent positive change, such as stopping smoking. Avoiding uncomfortable job search strategies, such as networking with others or cold calling employers reflects our internal homeostatic need to protect oneself from rejection and denial. Imposed change, the kind we have little control over, such as an unexpected job loss will likely affect one's sense of balance and continuity. Therefore, one way to handle unpleasant change is to employ strategies that help overcome homeostatic resistance such as looking the tiger in the eye and risking a little self-confidence and esteem.

- **Overcoming Habits**

Is now the time to explore new boundaries? New interests? New choices? Have you a choice between staying in status quo and changing? Are you being held back by fear of the unknown? Many, if not most of us, feel frustrated with the present, but are also uneasy about creating a new future. How does one reconcile the quandary? Unless you can create a solution out of whole cloth, you may want to start by exploring the landscape around you. One of the best tools to start with is the Internet

The demand for information technologies, from word processing to complex database management will continue to expand. Core industries, such as healthcare and renewable energy, and hundreds of others like them, will continue to spawn smaller companies and smaller businesses. Although demand for products and services may be low, most employers share one thing in common: they need to find qualified workers who will respond to interesting jobs and who are motivated and capable of contributing their skills, talents, and technical know-how to meet the employer's needs.

☑ a Gallery of Contacts

- **Friends and Family**

Like peeling an onion, the first layer includes friends and family, those with whom you have close emotional ties and proximity.

- **Referrals**

Employees often refer friends and acquaintances to their employers. Whether the company has a bonus program or not, employee referrals are good for a company for two reasons. First, employees tend to referral people they know will make good employees. Second, employee referral hires tend to be lower in cost per hire than outside hires.

- **Supervisor Assistance**

Most supervisors are very willing to help employees who have been laid off, particularly their own employees. Although you may be hurt, disappointed, possibly fighting feelings of unfair treatment, try to maintain contact with your former supervisor (if you are on speaking terms!). Having managed many such situations, I can tell you first hand that most manager's dread "reducing force." Whether to placate their sense of guilt for failing their employee, or for some other reason, there is a strong desire to help former employees find new employment. Experienced managers keep the lines of communication open in event of a potential recall. Furthermore, when managers provide help and show empathy, those emotional gestures, help guard against unlawful termination lawsuits. Remember also that you many need your former supervisor to provide an employment reference. Building a network beyond close, personal friends requires links with new employers and others, such as Human Resources.

- **Human Resources (HR)**

If a company is public, with stockholders, US Security Exchange Commission law requires that public companies publish the names and titles of their executives. On the other hand, privately held companies are not obligated to comply with SEC laws on disclosure. No guarantee, but one way around privately held information is to contact Human Resources. If the company has an HR department, one of their representatives may provide great information about job opportunities. How HR handles your call will depend on their approach to unsolicited inquiries. Instead, they may simply request you send your inquiry to the corporate applicant management system.

If you have a specific job in mind and HR does accept your call, you could ask the HR representative to clarify essential job requirements. You might try something like, *"The ad mentions marketing experience. Would six years' conference marketing qualify?"* HR's answer could open a good two-way dialogue.

☑ **Community Sanctuaries**

Many community resources provide counseling and transition assistance, and plain old emotional support. Public municipal, state, and federal agencies, and many private, community-supported non-profits, are available to everyone.

- **Senior Facilities**

Senior community centers are quickly becoming technology centers. No longer simply places for senior citizens, adult centers are hosting a variety of classes in information technology. Classrooms are complete with computers, up-to-date software programs, and wireless Internet connections. Companies are training their employees at senior centers, and subjects include word-processing, spreadsheet applications, email, and presentation graphics. Senior facilities are undergoing subtle, but significant changes in order to sustain themselves financially and to meet today's workforce needs.

- **Employment Centers**

Employment counseling centers receive funding based on numbers of people they place into full-time jobs. They offer a variety of programs and support, including skills training and career development counseling. Often supported through various government grants, local employment centers supplement the services provided by the State Departments of Employment

- **Career Education Centers**

Non-profit career education centers provide many transition services, ranging from one-on-one counseling to test administration and guidance. Governmentally and privately funded, local career education centers provide computers, printers, employer job databases, and Internet services. Their Boards of Directors are often comprised of local industry leaders.

- **Religious Facilities**

Many religious centers have set up job transition groups. Programs often include presentations by employers, human resource specialists, State Departments of Employment, and outplacement specialists. Religious centers maintain good contacts with community leaders and smaller business owners.

- **For-profit Training Centers**

Training companies offering classes in specialized training, such as customer service, communication skills, and business accounting, are a major source of newly trained workers for industry. These centers often advertise in local newspapers under, "training services." Specialized training companies represent a viable "bridge" to employment.

- **Volunteer Programs**

To fill a work gap or gain additional experience, volunteer work can create an employment advantage. Volunteer work provides numerous benefits, including assignment expertise, emotional attachment to a worthy cause, and contributions to a business mission, reminiscent of a private sector job. A volunteer assignment is no substitute for a paid job, but it can fill in the job gap. Although generally unpaid, volunteer work will help reduce feelings of isolation and anxiety from unemployment. For more on volunteering, visit volunteermatch.org. Use your interests, skills, and location to filter volunteer assignment listings.

- **State Departments of Employment**

Funded by state and federal governments, State Employment Departments assist workers with a variety of reemployment services. Although most jobs listed are non-management and senior professionals, those listed favor the local labor market of companies. Listing jobs with State Departments of Employment is one of the least costly sources for hires, particularly for smaller employers.

☑ Business Associations

Membership in business associations provides valuable networking opportunities and contacts. For this reason, you may want to search the Internet for 800 or 888 toll-free numbers to business associations of interest for membership information. Most associations provide membership lists for new enrollees, as well as access to their magazine and newsletters, current event schedules and professional development activities. More importantly, most professional associations list their members.

- **Industry Trade Associations**

Industry associations represent hundreds of disciplines, from the American Psychological Association (APA), to the Institute for Electronic and Electrical Engineers (IEEE), and are an important source of employment opportunities. In addition to networking, professional associations offer committee and volunteer activities, and opportunities to network for jobs.

Trade associations support a wide spectrum of industries, from automobiles to healthcare. Trade conventions feature industry products, services, as well as technical presentations, and the opportunities to mix with employers. Trade shows and trade conferences are a great way to learn about different industries and state-of-the-art products and services.

- **Technical Professional Sites**

Only one of many technical professional websites, Electrical Engineers can join the IEEE (Institute of Electrical and Electronic Engineering) by visiting their site (http://careers.ieee.org]. The IEEE, for example, provides career resource information suitable for college-level students, as well as experienced engineers. Like so many other technical professional sites, the IEEE provides resume-listing services, job fairs, job search tools, advice, and "links" to member company home pages.

- **Licensed Business Practitioners**

Licensed professionals, such as accountants, lawyers, or human resources specialists are sources of employment leads. Taking the initiative to network with licensed practitioners and business professionals can be a goldmine. On the other hand, contacting these individuals without a referral can take some nerve. Making "cold" or unsolicited contacts involves unexpected, occasional "brush offs." However, in my experience, most contacts are generous with their guidance. It is easier said than done, but don't let a case of nerves keep you from reaching out to a potential opportunity.

☑ Job Advertisements

- **Traditional Media Ads and On-line Postings**

Employers use traditional advertising to generate an immediate flow of applicants. The upside to an ad in a newspaper, job flyer or on the Internet is that it represents a legitimate opening. The downside is competition. Of course, if you have the gift of clairvoyance, send your resume to the manager before he or she feels the need to advertise the opening. However, under ordinary circumstances, when it comes to timing a response to an ad, applicant pools count. If there's a soft applicant pool (one with many qualified applicants), you may want to delay your response until a week or so after the ad appears. Delaying a bit may improve your odds of having your resume reviewed for more than three to ten seconds. A strategic delay will allow the initial flurry of applicants to pass by the manager like a herd of cows.

- **"Blind Ads"**

Employers occasionally disguise their ads and themselves. When they do, they will use "blind" ads. Instead of a company address, a blind ad only supplies a city and P.O. Box number for the employer's advertising agency or local newspaper. They collect and forward resumes to the employer. Several reasons justify blind ads, including:

- *an upcoming termination, planned resignation, or anticipated reorganization*
- *a need for qualified applicants for an anticipated project or contract*
- *a key position will be vacant, which employers may not want known by the public*
- *limited human resource or administrative resources to handle the resume flow.*

Open and active advertisements identify employers by means of name, address, fax number, email, or website. Rarely is a telephone number provided unless an employer is desperate and needs an immediate supply of applicants. Employers control applicant flow in a couple of ways, including using the phrase, "Principles only." All that means is that employment agencies are not to submit candidates.

- **Compliance with Employment Law**

Companies with 50 or more employees are required, under the Americans with Disability Act, to describe "essential duties and responsibilities" for positions, such as, "Senior Accountant." **Because different companies have different workforces, position descriptions and responsibilities will vary for the same job title.** Furthermore, corporate descriptions are often different from descriptions placed in ads for a number of reasons, not all fair, nor legal. Therefore, it is perfectly acceptable, although possibly a little annoying, for an applicant to call an employer, most often HR, to be clear about the essential duties and responsibilities advertised.

- **Ad Descriptions**

Employers advertise their openings using many different methods, from company websites to billboards, from newspapers to radio, and television, to online Internet postings, particularly through social media. During the early 1990s, many companies in California's Silicon Valley hired from a variety of sources, including billboards, radio, job fairs, newspaper advertising, and employment agencies. Although recruiting today has migrated toward the Internet and social networking, some managers still favor use of traditional newspaper advertising. If you decide to respond to a job advertised in the newspaper, be sure to follow a few simple rules. As an applicant, start by analyzing the ad's content, word-by-word, acronym-by-acronym, qualification by qualification. More specifically:

- **Ad Criteria**

When labor markets are soft, with many qualified applicants, ad criteria are strict. When labor markets are tight, with few qualified applicants, ad criteria are more flexible and accommodating. Those in engineering and information systems, for example, benefit from today's limited applicant supply. Too many jobs, too few applicants. To increase applicant flow, employers will loosen hiring standards and expand the applicant pool. Like any unsolicited brochure offering financial freedom and future success, job ads need careful screening to determine fact from fluff.

- **Soft Skills**

Between HR's review and the final ad, some managers will sneak in what is referred to as "soft skills," such as "strong communication skills," "ability to act in a team," "must be capable of adapting to a changing environment" or, that ever popular, "creative problem solver." It is no wonder applicants stare in disbelief! Applicants can only guess what an employer means, wants, or needs. My best advice is to read between the lines, toss a coin, and then guess what the employer wants. Nevertheless, underline the most important criteria, even the soft ones. Use a bit of ingenuity and clairvoyance to read between the lines. A cover letter or email is a good place to refer to a soft job requirement.

- **Strategic Delay Salary History**

Addressing an employer's request for salary history can be intimidating. For practical reasons, you may not want to give the employer salary data. If so, simply state in your correspondence or email that, "Salary history will be provided during negotiations." Delaying salary history until you have a good feel for a position's duties and responsibilities will improve your negotiating position.

☑ Recruiting Companies

When using an agency to represent you to employers, be sure to let any other employer know the agency or agencies you are working with. Likewise, let any agency you are working with know about the companies you have contacted. Transparency with employers and agencies will help avoid messy fee conflicts between companies and recruiting agencies. Always be clear about who is responsible for making contacts on your behalf. If an agency is not providing the kind of support you think you need, immediately cut your ties and send them a letter (versus an email) ending your relationship.

- **Contingency**

A contingent employment agency places permanent workers on a contingent basis. **They receive payment when their candidate is hired**. Fees for placing a candidate vary, but most often range twenty percent (or more) of the candidate's projected first-year income. Companies use contingent employment agencies when they are unable to fill positions using traditional methods, such as newspapers, online posting, job fairs, or employee referrals. Although contingent agencies fill a small number of jobs (3% to 5%), their services are important.

- **Retained Search**

Management initiates a retained search by having the retained search consultant to write a detailed position description. A retained search gives the executive search consultant the authority to represent their client. Unlike the contingency agency, retained search fees follow industry standards at thirty three and a half percent (33.5%), of the first year's anticipated employee compensation; which often includes hire-on bonuses, stock options, and special relocation benefits. Expenses are extra and final fees adjust when a candidate is hired. However, **unlike a contingent agency, retained search firms are paid an agreed upon fee even if a person is not hired**. For example, an executive salary of $200,000 would require a retained fee of $66,600 (33.3% of $ 200,000). Base fees exclude other expenses, such as travel, lodging, or psychological assessment costs. Only when all other recruiting methods are exhausted is a retained search consultant used. The decision to use retained search assignments resides with senior management.

- **Temporary Services**

Temporary employment services provide a solid alternative to regular full-time employment. Temporary for those who want work, can mean regular part-time 40 hours or less per week, short-term 8 hours per day, for several weeks or so, or occasional 8 hours or less per day, over varying times. Temporary employment can fill employment gaps created by cyclical or uncertain business cycles. Many temporary employment services provide some form of health insurance or other benefits to attract applicants. Some temporary agencies recruit only technical staff, whereas others may specialize in a particular discipline, such as accounting or construction. Most agencies post ads in "Yellow Pages" or online.

☑ Occupational Success in Motion

Perseverance leads to success. Wise use of time and energy is a good indication of perseverance. On average, most job seekers will spend two to four hours a day on job search activities. The time and energy you spend will depend on you. Because it is not mandated, you will need to find your own sense of perseverance and commitment. You will need to find your own level of energy.

- **Bumps and Spills along the Way**

Making a job or career change is bumpy, often random, and scary, like your first time on a roller coaster. One's Journey often enters the unknown, complete with unexpected turns, side excursions, and dead ends. More often than not, occupational journeys lead to new ventures, new jobs, and rejuvenated careers. **A job search, more specifically, *your* job search will likely include frustration, failures, and regrets—all par for the course**. The fact that you are contemplating this book's message, confirms several things: you are open to new strategies, that your self-confidence and sense of Resilience, continues to improve, and your optimism about your future is strengthening.

- **Action Overpowers Adversity**

Action over adversity has its benefits including feelings of accomplishment. Nevertheless, there is none more satisfying than that singular point where feelings of self-confidence, control, invincibility, and optimism mix, like a healthy, scrumptious ambrosia salad, creating a sense that your decisions, your strategies, your risks, have been on track all along, that your actions, perseverance and commitment are about to pay off. You have to remain focused on labor market trends and changes, changes to your resume, correspondence, face-to-face and Internet networking, pushing and convincing others to see you, and mapping new strategies that replace those that may have been ineffective in the past. This means that you have to circle back over past mistakes, noting new strengths and skills, and new insights. All of these activities, and more, lead to a zone where you begin to feel you are on the right track to success.

- **Success According to the Numbers**

Activities and numbers, if you plan to track them, are good, but may not be the best gauge of future success. Job and career success is not just about numbers. **Numbers have their place, but my advice is not to concentrate too much on numbers, such as the number of interviews, calls placed or resumes sent, but more on how you are feeling about your progress.** Set aside as much time as you think you need to mount a successful job search campaign, but be your own navigator. Avoid overworking, but try not to procrastinate. Take time to relax, regroup, and refresh before restarting your campaign.

☑ Another Option: Self-Employment

Shifting from the corporate world to entrepreneur is a dream for many. This shift takes confidence, resources, and extensive planning. A Web search will generate vast amounts of information on starting a business. Small Business Administration specialists (SBA.gov) offer substantial information on building a business. Another source of good information is SCORE. Their website, score.org, offers practical for advice on how to start or improve a business. **For shear quality of business information, you cannot beat professional and trade associations**. Joining professional associations that fit your vision may help you decide yes or no related to self-employment.

CHAPTER SEVEN

RESEARCH

Uncovering Career Opportunities

Internet (1970-1975)

Assisted by many computer scientists, the American, Vinton Cerf designed and created the original model of the Internet, building on his early research and experiments with packet-switching networks, supported by the U.S. Department of Defense Advanced Research Projects Agency. [Steve Johnson, *Where Good Ideas Come From*, p. 291]

Tools and Resources

The ability to explore job and career resources online is a marvel, thanks, in part, to the generosity of the US Government's Advanced Research Project Agency, better known as, DARPA.

DARPA's Brainchild

As the precursor to the Internet, DARPA established the Arpanet during the cold war with Russia, in large measure to protect crucial US government resources in the event of a nuclear attack. The Arpanet consisted of secured computer resources located at various major US universities, research, and military centers, thus creating the first web of computer sites. The public version of the Arpanet went live during the latter 1970s, and exits today as the worldwide web (www).

One of the benefits of the commercialization of the Internet has been its role in making available immense amounts of job and career resources. Although the Internet only fills seven to ten percent of all US jobs, it is still in its infancy as a job producer. Its potential is expanding with faster computer chips, cloud computing and with the proliferation of social networking. When it comes to research and resource mining, there is virtually no better means for than the Internet.

Given a computer, a word processor, and an online connection to the Internet, one can retrieve, dissect, parse, extract, cut, copy and paste information to one's heart content. Like a super fast dragster, with unlimited horsepower, control takes knowledge and skill to stay on track.

☑ Hyper Connections

In today's world of digital communications, access to information resources is crucial.

- **Wireless Technologies (Wi-Fi)**

Wireless technology makes the Internet available to anyone, anytime there is a connection: at virtually every gathering place, such as coffee shops, fast food restaurants, or the public library. Mobile communications, provided by Android, iPhone™ or iPad™, have taken communications to the universe. No wonder it is the perfect tool for searching job and career resources. At one's fingertips or the click of a mouse, one can search using a symbol, word or phrase, topic, company, trend, suggestion, or opinion. You name it; you can find it on the Internet. Wireless or hardwired, the Internet can put you in contact with a massive amount of information. Whether at home, or at a terminal in a library, or sipping coffee at Pete's, Internet connections open the gates to a storehouse of resources.

- **Cloud Computing**

Until recently, "cloud" was no more than a vague reference to a weather front. Now a common concept in computer lexicon, "clouds" of information float like large, overlapping Venn diagrams, providing vast amounts of information on demand, multiplied by linking computers made available by companies releasing excess computer storage and operating capacity. Capacity, storage, and computing power has taken a giant leap into digital space, and is now commonly referred to as "cloud computing." To us, the user, the cloud simply means greater and faster access to job and career information.

☑ The Savvy Researcher

Quick Tips

- *Read available Help pages*
- *Check spelling of search words and phrases*
- *Use capitalization if the search engine is case sensitive*

- **Too much Information?** *Use Boolean AND logic. Add specific qualifiers, such as, "Honda," rather than simply, "cars."*
- **Too little Information**? *Add alternate terms, more words and synonyms, or expand your search by connecting words or phrases with the Boolean OR drop the least important concept (s). Use different search engines besides Google or Bing, such as ASK.com.*

Retrieving too much or too little information is frustrating. However, adding or subtracting qualifiers, such as a job title, company name, industry, or topic, can manage quality and quantity of information. Another more sophisticated means of controlling the search is though use of Boolean logic operands, like the word, AND.

- **Boolean Search**

It is helpful to know that most search engines default to Boolean logic. For example, the use of a plus sign (+) or negative (-) sign will broaden or restrict a search. For example, a minus sign (-) in front of a word will exclude the word from any search results. On the other hand, Boolean operands, such as the word, NOT, will eliminate web pages containing words not wanted. In addition to Boolean logic, hidden, internal software tools, such as those developed by Google and Bing, aid users in their quest for specific information.

☑ A Tutorial on how to search the Internet [www.Internettutorials.net]

Without some training, using tools such as a skill saw or a nail gun can have serious consequences. The same goes for the Internet. **A little training, such as the following tutorial, can save the user a lot of grief and frustration**. As great a research tool as the Internet is, without your hand on the controls, you might as well put it back in the tool chest. However, under the user's control, one can explore the Internet's vast resources without leaving the comfort of one's home, or a Starbucks coffee shop, or the comfort of your local library. The Internet its own universe of information, at one's fingertips. All it takes is an Internet connected computer.

- **Insects and Robots**

Like dogs on a leash, tethered to their owners, software insects and robots have a way of crawling into any space within the Internet. If visions of insects bother you (arachnophobia), hold onto your hat, because they are constantly moving about the Internet. If you could look inside the Internet, you might think you are looking at a bunch of pesky insects and roving robots, but what you would actually be seeing is a group of software programs, with cute, anthropomorphic names. **These special, coded creatures are Internet drones, crawlers, robots, worms, spiders, and information stackers (horse flies).**

Like explorers, these hidden software creatures roam the World Wide Web, traversing and swinging from link-to-link, collecting, and indexing pages, combining Web pages and files, serving the whims of users. Spiders search and retrieve information by relevancy, whereas, other software programs, such as **"Link Ranking" and "Semantic Term Matching," group search results into blocks of information that are relevant and interconnected**. Then, there are "Concept Categories, Domains, Sites, and Personalization Ranking," which use search history preferences to determine order and relevance of search results. These behind-the-scene robot programs search the Internet on your behalf. Moreover, although fast, furious, and fastidious, they are under control, harnessed by a half dozen or so Internet search engines.

- **Search Engines**

Much of a job hunter's work centers on search and retrieval of job information. Along with many program subroutines, Internet search engines retrieve information from the Internet, efficiently and effectively. Equivalent to the operating system in a computer, search engines, likewise, are in control, if you will, of the vast resources on the world wide net. **Internet search engines group into General, Meta, Vertical, Blog, Social, and News**.

General

Google.com and **Google Directory.com**
Bing.com. Search engine
Ask. com. A general search engine enhanced by a dictionary, thesaurus, maps, news and more
Factbites.com. Searches full topic matches and returns full sentence excerpts.
Lycos.com. Searches deep Web content, including people searches, and yellow pages
SnappyFingers.com. Searches Frequently Asked Questions (FAQs) for answers queries
Mashpedia. Real-time results mix Wikipedia with news, videos, images, and Twitter messages
Wikipedia. A Web encyclopedia
Yahoo.com, and **Yahoo! Directory.com**
Meta Engines collect information from other search engines. Duplicates eliminated
Dogpile.com. Collates information by topic clusters, organized by keywords in the search

Zuula.com. Searches images, news, blogs, and job postings, configured in tabs

43 Marks.com. Searches, bookmarks: aggregates RSS (Really Simple Syndication) news, blogs, and other content available to users

Cacti Search.com. Cacti searches Google, Yahoo, MSN and Ask

MetaCrawler.com. combines results from Google, Bing, Yahoo!, and Ask

SortFix.com. Searches Google, Bing, and Bing Images, Twitter and YouTube Drag

Vertical Engines Retrieve specific subjects, such as industries and jobs

BizNar.com. Searches the world of business

IBoogie.com. Sorts results by categories and concepts

Hakia.com. Searches Internet using words that are semantically associated

Blog Engines include a number of sites, including:

Google Blog Search

Technorat.com. Indexes blog directories

Social Network Engines search social network programs, including:

Twitter Search.com and TweetScan.com

FriendFeed.com searches political commentary and other activities, such as travel

News Engines search news content, by subject, such as labor economics

Alltop.com

NewsNow.com

☑ Employment Databases

Without a doubt, the Internet is difficult to resist. It is beguiling, immensely appealing, a virtual storehouse of endless facts, statistics, solutions, and resources, including almost unlimited job and career possibilities. **Nevertheless, no matter how much you admire the Internet's power and potential, it will never manufacture a job or career path**. Furthermore, as much as one would like to buddy up to a perfect surrogate, the Internet is not smart enough to hammer out a resume, sweat through a tough interview, or construct a new career path. Unlike the mythical genie, that grants every wish, do not look to Internet to grant you a pass on tackling the arduous task of exploring the world of work.

• Job Sites

As the integrated computer chip increases in power, and industry continues to evolve amid cloud computing and social networking, so will go commercial employment sites. More than ever, change agents (counselors, educators, and employment specialists) rely on the Internet for ideas and solutions for their clients facing career issues where personality, interests, and experience are paramount to achieving occupational success. Although not all commercial employment sites cater to change agents and those seeking employment, some sites combine resume and employment services, whereas other commercial sites specialize in career advice and resume writing. **Some commercial services provide job advertising and resume prescreening, whereas other sites specialize in employment events, such as online job fairs.**

- **Websites of Choice**

The following mainstream social networking websites represent only a few, out of hundreds of sites that are available to job seekers. At last count, there were over three hundred established social networking sites, and more are emerging every day. Because sites constantly upgrade to encourage more users and improve their ease of use, it is always smart to check on their latest and greatest improvements. If you are, or will be using social networking, determine the most relevant two or three sites, before investing precious time and effort.

LinkedIn. www.linkedin.com. LinkedIn is a major site for job seekers, with millions of users and climbing. This site is also used by employer recruiters and staffing consultants. LinkedIn provides a URL (linkedin.com/in/yourfullname) and an "avatar," which best represents the user. Take full advantage of LinkedIn by distilling your objective into a tight mission statement.

Jobster. www.jobster.com. Experts in the use of Jobster see it as a platform for networking with employers. For example, one can upload a profile, embed a video resume, and highlight links to one's personal site. A personal picture, along with skill tags, can also be included. The functionality is there, just be frugal with personal information.

MyWorkster. www.myworkster.com. MyWorkster networks employers with college students and alumni. Users create professional profiles for employers interested in recruiting those with degrees in specific disciplines, such as engineering or biology.

Ryze.com. This site links business professionals, particularly new entrepreneurs. Ryze claims to have over 500,000 members, in 200 countries, with over 1,000 external organizations hosting sub-networks, with paid and unpaid memberships. This is a site to consider if you want to spread your wings.

Tribe.com. This site networks people with common interests. Users connect according to categories, such as alumni/schools, companies, co-workers, computers and Internet, and family & homes.

Professionals market their business with press releases, blogs, and event notices. Connecting with others with similar interests and spinning your interest in a job takes some skill, but it may all be worth it.

Twitter. www.twitter.com. A strange, but popular 140-word maximum communication device, Twitter users can "tweet" directly with others, including hiring managers. Once "connected" with another tweeter, in a particular industry or company, it is easy to connect with "movers and shakers" in your area of interest. Search wefollow.com for a directory of tweeters organized by interests

Facebook. www.facebook.com. There are two main ways of acquiring a job through Facebook. First, go to the Facebook marketplace, which lists job openings, then, message the hiring manager or join groups and "fan" pages of users with similar interests. Avoid posting anything "goofy." Some employers are sensitive and opinionated. Use good judgment

☑ Internet Social Networking

In spite of ethical conflicts, vulnerabilities to misuse, and privacy issues, trends appear clear: job seekers and recruiters have teamed up, to use social networking to their mutual advantage. For example, Facebook, in partnership with the US Department of Labor, has rolled out an application (app) listing roughly two million openings that one can search by key word type of work, industry, and location. Some job seekers consider social networking daunting. Others, such as writers, use social networking as their most important marketing strategy, to target and reach their reading audience. Job seekers can apply the same marketing strategies.

- **Benefits, Trends and Surveys**

For all its sins, social networking serves as one of the great inventions of our time. As members of the human race, we have always known that we share a common bond. **Nonetheless, it took the advent of online social networking to prove the point. Industry surveys strongly suggest that social networking is another way to create a bond with employers**. Therefore, another path to finding the source of employment opportunities is through social networking, and employers like it. Employers who hire from social networks are able to reduce their recruiting costs per hire (CPH), by ten to fifteen percent. Multiply that cost reduction by several hundred hires and the CPH savings are impressive. Hires from social networks not only lower recruiting costs, they improve the bottom line and higher revenues.

A 2013 member survey conducted by the National Society of Human Resource Managers (SHRM.org), focused on "Social Networking Websites and Recruiting/Selection." The survey determined a number of pluses and some minuses for using social networking to recruit. The number one plus was access to passive job applicants (80%), whereas the number one reason for avoiding using social networking to recruit was, "Concerns about legal risks," associated with accessing protected information, such as age, race, gender, religious affiliation and so on. Recruiters used LinkedIn the most (94%). SHRM reported several important findings, including greater competitive edge, and increased employer brand recognition. **SHRM's survey also found that most employers do not use social networks to screen candidates, nor are their policies in keeping with the proliferation of the use of social websites to recruit.**

The 2012 Jobvite.com Survey of 1,000 Recruitment Specialists established that social networking is changing how recruiters find and hire applicants. The survey found that roughly:

92% of recruiters use or plan to use social recruiting

43% of recruiters who use social recruiting have seen an increase in candidate quality

73% of recruiters in the survey have successfully hired a candidate through social networking

31% of recruiters using social networks have seen a sustained increase in employee referrals.

Jobvite concluded: "*Job seekers believe they have a better chance to land a job if they are connected, proactive, and prepared-and rightly so. These are some of the very qualities employers look for when hiring, and social networks are emerging as the meeting ground for like-minded innovative employers and prospective employees.*"

☑ **Partnership with Employers**

Human resources specialists and private recruiting agencies constantly source for applicants from social networks, thereby extending their reach to applicant pools. By doing so, they are taking advantage of the symbiotic relationship that exists between the applicant and their "membership" in various social networks. A corporate recruiter's incentive, therefore, resides in fact that sourcing applicants from social networks produces lower costs per hire. Furthermore, even though it may seem counter intuitive, but the more senior the position, the more likely recruiters will use online sourcing. Use of social networks produces good results for employers and applicants alike. Nevertheless, seasoned recruiters know that no one recruitment source provides everything they need. What recruiting strategy works for executives will not necessarily work for truck mechanics. Nevertheless, it is abundantly clear that use of Internet social networking will come to dominate the recruiting process. **Several surveys support the premise that a significant number of recruiters and applicants have and will benefit from using social networking to find their next job.**

☑ Unintended Exposure

Social profiles are open books for employers who judge applicants based on their social network page. What you display reflects your state of being, polished, or silly looking. Ask yourself; what kind of profile you want the public to see. Whatever your friends can see, so can an employer. A rule of thumb: if you are going to use social networks as a part of your job search campaign, make sure your posting reflects a professional image. **An applicant risks turning off potential employers by posting images of you partaking at a bong party.**

- **Loss of Privacy**

We all seem to struggle with privacy issues, including employers. Our precious privacy is the last thing we want to lose. However, employers think they are entitled to all information, whereas the applicant feels differently. Employment people seem to devour information on applicants. And, why not? A bad hire does not sit well with management. However, privacy is important to all of us. We like to act silly, even bizarre, at times. Nevertheless, because virtually everyone hired goes through a background check, what better way for an employer to vet an applicant than to scour an applicant's social website. Not everyone agrees with the notion of unfettered intrusion. **A recently enacted law in California restricts employers from asking applicants for their social site access. I agree, but not every state agrees with me.**

Employers in California can still ask for an applicant's social site, but they cannot make it a condition of employment. Therefore, make it a rule: do not post extraneous, personal information on your social site that may cause unintended consequences and damage to your chances for a great job. Political views, for example, may influence a biased manager. What goes for politics goes for other personal information, such as hobbies and avocations, like sky diving, or group affiliations, such as Hell's Angels membership, or even medical conditions, such as visual or hearing loss. All of these extraneous personal revelations may turn off a biased manager.

- **Intrusion and Fraud**

On the one hand, social networking has opened another door to human-to-human communication. **On the other hand, social networking has opened a Pandora's Box of Internet vulnerabilities**

making it easy for those who harbor sinister motives. Pandora's Internet Box has released into the public domain those who want to steal your privacy, exploit the innocent, and commit fraud. Personal information, once protected, is no longer as safe as it once was. Granted, social networking opens doors to human connectivity, but also creates opportunities for nefarious hackers, who are looking to exploit unwary social network users. Intruders and hackers team up to perpetrate computer crimes using information from social network pages. It is a sad commentary, but exploiting social interaction is the hacker's dream.

- **Sociological Dilemmas**

The "www" has created intriguing sociological dilemmas, for applicants and employers alike. However, in spite of these ethical dilemmas, employers continue to value job seekers who use social networks to hunt for jobs. **Social networking is not only strategically advantageous for applicants; it is also advantageous for employers.**

- **Employer Policies**

Posting one's resume on a commercial resume database, such as monster.com, may not breach an employer's policy, but it may, nevertheless, raise eyebrows if noticed. Therefore, practice good judgment in deciding when and where to post your resume to a job site. As you are posting your resume to a particular site, your employer may be searching the same site for applicants with backgrounds similar to yours. Some employers will take umbrage with an employee looking for work on company time, whereas other employers may be more lenient. Monster.com recognizes the human tendency to look for greener pastures, and offers those who use their site the option of blocking employers, their own or others, from viewing and retrieving their resume.

- **Corporate Restrictions**

Corporate policies cover virtually every major subject affecting employee behavior, particularly policies affecting use of the Internet during work hours. **Using social networks or searching restricted employment sites may conflict with corporate policy**. Violating corporate policy could result in termination or prosecution, at worst, or embarrassing corporate backlash, at least. Spend personal Internet time outside of work.

- **Firewalls**

Although employers actively source social network sites for applicants, they often use software that "firewalls" employees from accessing the same Internet sites during work hours. It may not seem fair, but employers have the upper hand when it comes to their policies. In addition to employer firewalls, a number of institutions protect proprietary information and web pages from public search. Information licensed to libraries and affiliated users, for example, is frequently concealed behind password-protected sites, classified information databases, and e-journals.

- **Applicant Management System (AMS)**

Nothing is more frustrating to an applicant than discovering that a particular posting has been filled, deleted, or simply rewritten to reflect a change in duties and responsibilities. Likewise, out-of-date job postings (or anything else for that matter) cause problems for employers, as well. **Everyday employers post thousands of jobs, but often fail to keep them current**. I have been there and it is tough to keep job openings up to date. Furthermore, applicants, who are later hired, often remain in the applicant database because resume profiles do not automatically transfer over to the employment database. It is common for more than one employer to retrieve the same applicant because an applicant's resume may reside in more than one employer's database. In addition, software platforms (SAP vs. Oracle, for example) **run applicant and employee databases on different operating platforms, making transfer of files from one database to another impossible**.

☑ Library Resources

In addition to computers and Internet resources, do not forget your local library. **Internet resources are a wonderful indispensible tool, but libraries provide a wealth of additional support and informational resources.** Most libraries provide dedicated professionals who are there to help direct you to mountain of information. A librarian's support can make the difference between confusion and enlightenment. Most libraries include wonderful directories, such as the following.

- *The Standard Periodical Directory*. This directory provides an index of weekly and monthly Periodicals, such as *Business Week, Forbes, Fortune, New York Times*, and the *Wall Street Journal*.
- *The Directory of Manufacturers* sorts manufacturers by industry. *The Directory of Directories* is a compendium of directories.

- *The Encyclopedia of Associations or the Directory of Associations* provides information on thousands of associations in the United States.
- The *US Industrial Outlook*, or *Standard and Poor's Industry Survey*, for US and International business trends.
- *The Encyclopedia of Managerial Job Descriptions, Dictionary of Occupational Titles*, and the *Occupational Outlook Handbook,* are available online
- *Chambers of Commerce*, in most cases, will sell their member directory for a small fee. Chamber Members are generally sorted by location, product, or service, along with names and contacts for owners and executives.
- *Niche directories.* Recruiting firms use to source applicants, most often from publicly traded corporations. Most of these special directories come in limited quantities and can cost up to several thousand dollars per edition.

☑ Government Information Sites

- **Department of Labor Database of Positions (http://online.onetcenter.org)**

The US Department of Labor (DOL.gov) Occupational Information Network (O*NET), contains a virtual cornucopia of job information. The DOL's database for 800 positions includes a one-stop source of information, such as: job type, duties and responsibilities, tools used, including software programs; US and Regional pay rates, which are important to the job hunter negotiating an offer; related jobs, personality features for each job, and the education and experience generally required for each position.

- **Standard Industrial Classification (SIC.gov)**

For a view into the vast range of US industries, look no further than the Standard Industrial Classification, known as the SIC (SIC.gov). The SIC groups industries by four-digit codes, which are further expanded by the six-digit North American Industry Classification System (NAIC.gov). Private, public, and governmental agencies use both systems to classify their businesses and their employees. The Securities and Exchange Commission (SEC.gov), for instance, uses the SIC system to report economic data for more than 400 industries and sub-industries. The SIC is constantly updated with new industries and new technologies

- Investment Stock Fund Prospective

A terrific way to target companies by industry or business type is to search mutual fund prospectuses. Simply Google, "fund prospectus" to retrieve hundreds of mutual fund prospectuses. For example, Fidelity Investments and Teachers Annuity Association and College Retirement Equity Fund (TIAA-CREF), group publicly traded companies by industry, from aerospace to defense, from solar energy to petroleum. Take your pick, any industry, or any company that strikes your fancy. However, for the best use of your time and energy, focus on industries and companies of immediate for potential interest. Once you have a company in mind, the next step is research.

- **Search Example**

If the SIC is not enough, one can search for particular companies by industry. For example, the search phrase, *"list companies providing healthcare software"* produces hundreds of "hits" or references to the subject and links from hits to other sites. The cited search phrase produces hundreds of hits including the following two searching for healthcare software companies.

"**LIST HEALTHCARE SOFTWARE COMPANIES**" will produce many citations and links to healthcare.

"This is an extensive **list** of **companies** developing **software** solutions for the . . . **Provides** a variety of **healthcare** management **software** solutions for the *www.usmetros.com/weblinks/healthcare_ software.htm* Cached—Similar"

Health Care Software Business Directory—Find Health Care . . .

Below find a list of all **companies** in this industry: **Health Care . . .** Claricode provides software development to **healthcare** providers, medical. . . . *www.pr.com Computers & Software › Computer Software*—Cached—Similar"

☑ Unlimited Research

As the Internet continues to evolve, its singular use as a job and career strategy is also still maturing. **The future task remains for employment algorithms to be able to match an applicant's personality, interests and experience to employment needs**. Moreover, until that day arrives, we will continue to waste vast amounts of untapped labor market resources.

- **"2001: A Space Odyssey's Hal"**

Relying on the Internet for direction is, in some ways, like relying on Hal, the computer savant in the science fiction movie, *2001: A Space Odyssey*. Like Hal, the Internet, has the answers, but refuses to provide the solutions. Without a sense of purpose and direction, the Internet may overwhelm the user with too much information, likely hindering a job search rather than facilitating solutions.

Instead of spending endless hours on the Internet, digging for answers in bottomless storehouses of information, refocus your initial direction and purpose. Revisit your sense of who you are and how you want others to see you. Recheck your interests to make sure they are in line with your marketing campaign. **Finally, link your resume of work experience to your campaign and to your interests.** Ask yourself if they reinforce one another. Research tools, like the Internet, are only as good as the control their users exert over them.

As a research tool, the Internet is front and center, but its value is in your hands of the user. What is the value of unlimited access to mountains of information if the results are directionless? **It is a fact using the Internet can be downright exhausting, unless you start your search with a plan, any kind of plan.**

CHAPTER EIGHT

RESUMES

Ticket to the World of Work

Resume: a written exaggeration of only the good things a person has done in the past, as well as a wish list of the qualities a person would like to have. [Bo Bennett]

A short descriptive summary, as of events. An account of the author's personal experiences. Autobiography—a biography of yourself.

The Employment Resume: Past, Present, and Future

The employment resume should cover one's past, present, and future occupational goals, in one or two pages. The resume serves a number of purposes, but mostly as one's employment history. Although a snap shot of one's personality, interests and experience, writing a resume sounds easy on paper, but is anything but. Moreover, although the resume is one of the most important occupational strategies, it is one of the least favorite tasks. This Chapter tells how and why deft use of words and language can help create a resume worthy a king's ransom.

☑ Fundamentals to Writing a Compelling Resume

Whether for the first or the tenth time, creating a resume can be a challenge. You can use the help of online resume templates and professional resume writers, but they are secondary to the personal touch. Nevertheless, there are no slam-dunks, no short cuts, no stand-ins, or substitutions. **Writing a compelling resume is tough work**.

Resumes often suffer the effects of procrastination and benign neglect. It is not much of an exaggeration to say that many, not counting yours, look quilt-like, made by Grandma, loosely sown together with scraps of outdated job descriptions. If you want your resume "tossed" in the nearest trashcan, this is the way to do it. Moreover, turning the job of writing the resume over to a so-called resume "expert," may not be much of an answer either.

Consider your resume a mirror. The image changes as you change. Once a month, or once a year, it is smart to update your resume to reflect who you are, what you want, and what you have done. A look in the mirror can be very motivating.

[**Warning**: *Count on rewrites, frustration and perseverance. Interesting, compelling resumes are works in progress. However, before putting pen to paper, take a moment to think how you are going to make your resume persuasive, one that compels the reader to hang on each word, intrigued with your jobs and accomplishments, with your contributions, commitment and promise. To that end, consider the impact of semantics, the power words, and language when put into action.*]

☑ Resume Formats

Whether it's a resume, memoir, or autobiography, writers share one thing—they want the reader's attention. Be it an audience of one manager, or a panel of six interviewers, you want those with the authority to hire to want to read your resume. You want the reader's undivided attention on what you have written about your personality, interests, and experience. However, getting their attention is not easy. To do so will require a little razzle-dazzle and enough buzzwords, and acronyms to grab the reader's attention. Your first step, then, is to choose a resume format that best fits your background and purpose. Resumes come in three formats: *Chronological, Functional and Hybrid*. **No resume is perfect. All these resume formats have their pluses and minuses, depending on one's background, intended audience, and what is to be accomplished.**

Although there is no hard and fast rule, a two-page resume is generally sufficient, for a couple of reasons. First, two pages should accommodate for roughly ten years of experience. Second, and most importantly, employers are largely not interested in receiving more than two pages of resume, nor more than roughly ten years experience. Finding the balance between page spacing and resume content is tricky. Be prepared to write and rewrite your work history until it looks and feels like you.

• **Personal Choice**

Are you going to sail your resume over the oceans of work using a *chronological, functional, or a hybrid* format? Are you going to use a chronological format for one employer and a hybrid for another? Are you going to format your resume to fit every opening, every situation, and every manager? Is your prior experience sufficient, or are you going to concentrate on your most recent jobs? Are you going to cover more than ten years experience or just the last several jobs? Are you concerned about revealing your age? How do you plan to express your sense of optimism and confidence? Have you given any thought as to how are you going to market your resume? These are questions to consider before roughing out a first resume or revising your current resume.

If you have fewer than ten years experience, for instance, you will most likely use the traditional, chronological format, where you list your recent job first. On the other hand, if you have more than ten years experience, you may want to drop the older experience, or, consider using a functional or the hybrid format. For versatility, use the functional and/or hybrid resume. They offer greater flexibility, but require more creativity. The chronological format remains the accepted standard.

▤ Chronological

Chronological resumes list jobs by date, current or most recent first. Most resumes, whichever format, start with name, address, phone number(s), email address, or other contact information.

Sample Chronological Resume Format

Ralph Smith

rm12345@ispcast.net

Cell 100-444-3434

Experience Summary: [The summary statement is a brief overview of key strengths. Good summary statements correspond to a company's needs.]: **Marketing professional with over ten years experience in sales management.**

Objective: [Not every resume writer uses an objective, but if you do, tailor it to companies or jobs of interest. If using a cover letter, consider adding your job objectives to your summary statement.]

Entry-level position in electronics sales
Manufacturing manager for children clothing
Loan officer for a community bank
Sales manager for a residential security systems manufacture
Employment History

Begin the employment history with, "Experience," "Business Background," or "Professional Experience." Your call. For each employer, provide a job description, and, if possible, a contribution or two. List your work contributions (responsibilities) in order of importance.

Special Skills and Education

Use this area to cite special training, seminars, and or workshops, such as computer programming, spreadsheet or presentation applications. List your highest college degree first, if you have one. Cite your college or university and its location. Abbreviations like "AS, "BA" or "MS," are common. Avoid the year of your degree, if you are forty or older.

Military Service—Security Clearances

Military service is important to some employers. In addition, most Department of Defense and defense contractors require security clearances. US agencies or defense contractors often include the requirement for security clearance in their employment ads.

Functional resumes group skills and experience under broad headings, such as "Leadership," "Communications," or "Technical Expertise." The functional format works well for those with extensive experience or conversely, minimal experience. Those with college or special training but little work experience could use headings, such as, "Quantitative Skills," "Customer Communications," or "Volunteer Service" to cover non-work experience. Although an accepted format for consultants, most employers are uncomfortable with functional resumes because, although they cover broad, functional experience and expertise, it is sometimes difficult to match functional experience with specific employers.

🗐 Hybrid

Sometimes, neither the chronological nor the functional format fits the bill. The hybrid format, on the other hand, combines the chronological and functional resume. The hybrid resume uses roughly the top third of space to include functional contributions, under headings like, "Management Communications" and the remaining space for the chronological work history, which can include dates and names of employers.

Although designed to be flexible, the hybrid format does run the risk of looking a bit fragmented and disorganized. Some managers have reservations about functional or hybrid resumes in that they feel the applicant may be trying to hide or disguise their specific work history. Unless you have a good reason to use the hybrid format, I recommend you stay with the chronological format.

☑ Words, Maps, and Territories

According to Alfred Korzybski, pioneer in the field of general semantics, when we process what we see and hear, we are creating neurological "maps", that are analogous to maps that represent real, corresponding territories. According to Korzybski, we organize our world by mapping our interpretation to reality. For some, the match is highly accurate, but not for all. Then again, we know they are no perfect matches. In his book, *Language in Thought and Action*, S.I. Hayakawa, another semanticist, described the process of mapping in the following way: "*Gradually, maps which we have inside our heads become fuller, more accurate pictures of the actual territories of human character and behavior.*" The principle of mapping applies in the same way to one's resume. What a manager reads from a resume becomes their neurological map of applicant's job experience. **Your goal, then, is to make sure your resume maps as much as possible with your personality, interests, and experience.**

- **Levels of Abstraction**

S.I. Hayakawa points out that clear, accurate communication "*requires the constant interplay of higher and lower levels of abstraction*" (pg. 135). Applying Hayakawa's advice means using specific words language to define abstract work responsibilities to specific, concrete contributions. **Connecting work results to responsibilities and accomplishments will inject a sense of action and purpose into your resume.** Concentrating on what you have contributed, the goals you have met, and objectives you have achieved, will push your resume to the front of the line. An abstract list of duties and responsibilities will float in the ethers until tethered to Planet Earth by specific contributions.

- **Grabbing Attention**

Without a sense of action and direction, a resume will go nowhere fast. Weak resumes are bound for the trash heap. On the other hand, combining action words with well-crafted work results has the potential to grab the reader's attention. When written beyond the usual one-dimension collection of dates, places, and names, a resume can be brought back to life by creating an interesting personality, with coherent interests, and relevant experience. Getting there does not come easily, and it is hard work.

Careful use of action words can compel a reader to stop, look and take notice. This is what you want. You want your contributions to jump off the page into his or her stream of consciousness. You want the employer to read your resume and then to ask themselves how you accomplished that particular task, or that certain responsibility, or how was it that you knew to act decisively? You want the employer to wonder who sees you as reliable and why? In what ways did you help or lead the team? How was it that you mediated a disagreement with another department? What methods did you use to coach new employees? You want the employer to ask themselves questions that only you can answer, preferably over the phone or better, yet, during a face-to-face interview.

- **Injecting Action Words**

Injecting action words into one's experience can bring life to one's work history. Moreover, there is no better way to highlight one's work contributions or experience than to use action verbs to breathe life into a lifeless resume. Using words, such as *expedited, initiated, created,* and *organized* are just a few of hundreds of action verbs that can bring strength to one's work experience.

☑ Link Your Message to Your Resume

Interesting, exciting books, articles, stories and poetry, those that touch our emotions and inspire us, require well-crafted use of words and language that reflect strength of personality, interests and experience. **A writer's goal, your goal, is to get the reader to visualize you - your sense of optimism, personality, interests, qualifications, and capabilities.**

- **Vitality with Action Words**

Action verbs, or power words, infer strength and vitality. Luckily, the English language is chock-full of words that cause a reader to infer action. **Action words can inject life into a boring, lifeless resume. They have the power to convert bland corporate job descriptions into compelling snapshots of employment history.** For example, the job duty, ". . . *worked with cash flow statements*" is, by any stretch of the imagination, pretty bland. However, when rewritten as, "*audited cash flow statements which improved fund balances by 45 percent,*" the applicant's job duty is a lot more intriguing. It may even prompt the reader to ask him or herself, "How in the world did they improve fund balances by 45% by simply auditing?" The invigorated image suggests that the applicant possibly has the ability to improve the auditing function for the manager.

Action verbs infuse initiative, power, and vitality into lifeless work descriptions. Whenever possible, use action words like bait, to catch a reader's attention. Set yourself aside from others. Write your resume with the goal of compelling the reader to "visualize" who you are.

- **Passive Words and Wilted Contributions**

Passive words in work statements connote obedience. Great for a dog, but not what one wants in a resume. Words such as *assist, help, support, serve, provide, relieve, supply, deliver, furnish, participate*, do not bode well if you are trying to create a picture of vitality, enthusiasm, assertion, initiative, and conviction. If you decide to describe your work using passive words, tie the work activity to a finished product or contribution. For example, "I helped deliver fifteen tons of aluminum scrap by hand to a recycling center."

☑ Contributions that Speak Volumes

Most applicants are generally satisfied with their resumes, when it comes to concentrating on dates, places, duties, and responsibilities. The top of the resume contains their name, but the body and substance of their resume appears disconnected. One might say gruesome. Many applicants cannot seem to get their resumes to look connected. **When asked, most applicants will answer that their resumes "just do not seem to capture who I am." Most resumes do a good job covering what was done, but a poor job communicating what was accomplished**. After many rewrites, an applicant may eventually come to the realization that simply cutting and pasting job descriptions into one's resume leaves out the most important ingredient—results and contributions.

Effective use of words, whether a bestselling whodunit, or a killer resume, translates ideas into visual images. In other words, connecting abstract responsibilities to descriptive results will improve a resume to the nth power. Your resume should be more than a series of places and dates; it should compel the reader to stop in their tracks to make a personal connection, beyond someone else's corporate job description. A collection of job duties and responsibilities says everything, yet nothing about the job's outcome, or its contribution to the success of the company. You have seen them before, corporate job descriptions contain everything under sun, but rarely state performance expectations, contributions or results. As it turns out, results are the flint that sparks a reader's connection.

☑ **Compelling Resumes**

Many, if not most of us, have little idea what effect our work has had on an employer's success. Why? Because most employees fail to link their employee's work contributions to measures of success. This oversight omits one of the most important ingredients or a compelling resume. Unless a manager quantifies goals for their employees, subtle, important contributions will be forgotten, unappreciated, or simply ignored, or unrecognized. However, in spite of this failing, it is important, no, very important, that you try to bridge your work history with some measure of results and contributions.

Writing a concise, compelling resume is challenging, for the best of writers. However, aside from the use of crafted words and language, one can dramatically improve her or his resume by using four components of strong work description. Each component carries with it its own power to strengthen a work description with the use *action words, task descriptions, times to complete a job, and the finished results.*

Action   **action verbs and power words**
Task   **duties/responsibilities/tasks**
Time   **time used to complete a task, a program, a goal**
Results   **end product/result/accomplishment/outcome/solution**

It is natural for a manager to compare an applicant's work contributions to the opening. It is also natural for the manager to compare the applicants work to his or her own experience. **Therefore, there is no better way to inspire interest in one's resume than to describe work results in measurable standards, such as time, cost, expense, revenue, income, profits, proceeds, earnings, and so on**. If you want or need to strengthen your resume, consider each contribution in terms of results. With a little work, you can greatly improve your resume, thereby improving your credibility and promise as a future employee.

- *Action Words*: **to the First Power**

Compelling resumes are more effective when work results start with action words. Beyond the physical appearance of a resume, you want to grab a reader's attention with a sharp jab to their senses. In other words, start with actions words that precede each work contribution, achievement, or accomplishment.

Note the following table. Two action words, "provided" and "developed" precede or modify task/responsibility. Look at your resume and make sure each of your contribution statements starts with an action word.

Action (Words)	Task/Responsibility
Provided	. . . guidance to twenty new staff members
Developed	. . . a wide area network for a 25-state region

- *Task/Responsibility*: to the 2nd Power

Kick the list off with your corporate job description. Drop the stuff that never applied, listing actual tasks or responsibilities for each job, by priority.

Action (Words)	Task/Responsibility
Donated . . .	. . . three days a week to helping children read
Designed . . .	. . . 25-item questionnaire to gauge customer service satisfaction

- *Time*: to the 3rd Power

Connecting completion times to work contributions is a powerful communication technique. Why? Because linking results by time, or any other quantitative measure, creates a neurological comparison between an applicant's contribution and a manager's experience. Mental comparisons result in mental connections. Moreover, mental connections result in more questions and interviews. Creating packets of accomplishments that are rich in information will strengthen neurological connections with the reader. Using the power of time as a measure of success is intellectually intriguing, like a silvery fly on the end of angler's hook. The manager may bite, nibble, or reject the applicant's experience, but the power of time has a way of making connections, and its connections that counts.

Action (Words)	Task/Responsibility	Time	Results
Instituted . . .	. . . a marketing program for a brand shampoo in major international magazines . . .	. . . over a corresponding three-month period . . .	. . . that drew in more than 5,000 responses resulting in a 22 percent sales increase
Designed . . .	. . . a product logo for a medical products group . . .	. . . under a tight six month deadline . . .	. . . that resulted in a six major consulting assignments

☑ • Results: to the 4ᵗʰ Power

Describing work results using measures, such as dollars, units, volume, or percentages, will compel most managers to take notice, sparking a comparison to their own experience. Connections create attention.

Action (Words)	Task/Responsibility	Time	Results
Led . . .	. . . a project team to design the flow of materials in a manufacturing plant, that . . .	. . . within 60 days . . .	would produce a reduction in material waste by 120 percent
Raised . . .	. . . $1500 dollars for the alumni fund . . .	. . . in eight weeks . . .	exceeding the annual goal by 16 percent
Conducted . . .	. . . training sessions to . . .	. . . met a strict deadline to	. . . Inform managers of new legislation
Developed . . .	. . . marketing schedules for three separate health care products . . .	. . . over 2 weeks which . . .	. . . Improved market share by ten percent
Created . . .	. . . a database using SAP to update and obtain data . . .	. . . under a three-week deadline which cut . . .	. . . search-time by 50 percent
Revised . . .	. . . 120 job descriptions . . .	. . . within three weeks in order . . .	. . . to comply with the Americans with Disabilities Act

- Softer Powers

For sure, linking accomplishments by time or results will create a stronger, more compelling resume. **However, in some instances, linking results to values, such as money, volume, or percentages may be impossible.** For example, expressing improvement in morale may be difficult to quantify using numbers or percents. Nevertheless, there are other options. One could use words like, increased, or enhanced to connote an improvement in morale. Improvements in morale or customer satisfaction often intrigue managers because they are often accountable for the same work place conditions. Still, numbers and values are the best grabbers.

- A Lesson in Verbs, Nouns, and Adjectives

In a 1999 article, Richard Bolles described usage of **nouns** (persons, places, and things), **verbs** (action words), and **adjectives** (descriptors), as the pillar to compelling resumes.

Verbs (Action Words)	Nouns	Adjectives or Adverbs
Talents	Subject skills	Traits
Natural gifts	Knowledge words	How transferrable skills are used
Natural skills	"Expertise"	Created through experience

Examples	Examples	Examples
Programming	*Computers*	*Efficiently*
Writing	*MSWord*	*Concisely*
Negotiating	*ActiveX*	*Strategically*
Planning	*Designer*	*Effectively*
Analyzing	*Engineer*	*Adroitly*
Teaching	*English*	*Tactfully*

- Concise Work Descriptions

Crisp, clean, compelling resumes include well-written, concise, action-oriented work descriptions. If your experience is narrow, concentrate on quantifying results. If you cannot quantify results, focus on writing clear and concise duties and responsibilities.

☑ Practical Resume Tips

The perfect resume format does not exist. Some use wide margins, some narrow. Some use fancy fonts and bullets, or none at all. Whereas one resume format may appeal to one applicant or manager, the same format may distract others. Some resumes satisfy expectations in certain industries, such as graphics design, most resumes are generic. Besides misspelling a word or citing an incorrect date, there are other errors to keep in mind.

- **Hidden Glitches**

From a simple misspelling to the lack of a period, take the time to look carefully for nasty, hidden glitches. It is a fact that our brains process information so fast we often fill in the blanks on a page, where a word is skipped, or we miss a hidden glitch. Ask another person to read over your resume. A second set of eyes is better than one.

- **Employment Gaps**

Given today's recession, employment gaps are common, more the result of the recession than personal choice. However, in spite of reality, if you think the gap will stick out like a sore thumb, raise the issue before the interviewer asks. **Taking the initiative to call attention to a gap in employment presents a perfect opportunity to highlight one's perseverance in finding reemployment, an important quality to employers**. There are many acceptable reasons for employment gaps, including outsourcing of jobs, relocation of operations, business downsizing, reorganizations, consolidations, and so on. However, what you have been doing during the gap is more important. Be prepared to explain any job gaps, if with nothing more than actively looking for employment.

- **Proper Tenses**

It is easy to trip on improper tense usage. If currently employed, use the present tense in your resume. If not, use the past tense.

Present tense:	I fabricate machinery parts
Past tense:	My job required fabricating parts
Future tense:	My job will involve fabricating parts

- **Attaching Documents**

Employers are reluctant to accept resumes attached to emails, for fear of receiving viruses and/or malware. It is better to send a hard copy of your resume through the mail, or in the body of the e-mail, unless given permission to send it as an attachment. Otherwise, the manager will likely get a computer "pop up" message, warning such as:

"**Note:** *To protect against computer viruses, e-mail programs may prevent sending or receiving certain types of file attachments. Check your e-mail security settings to determine how attachments are handled.*"

Whatever method you use, be sure to introduce the reason for your inquiry, in the form of a brief introduction.

- **Video Resumes**

No doubt about it, videos resumes have a certain appeal. However, a video resume may show the good in you, but also the bad. There are a several reasons to rethink a video resume. First, Human Resource professionals generally discourage the practice. Secondly, most employers do not upload video resumes into their applicant management systems. **More importantly, video resumes often contain too much personal information, which may lead to inadvertent or overt discrimination**. The last thing you want is for an employer to make a decision based on personal features, such as appearance, age, race, gender, appearance, disability, or sexual and political orientation.

However, If you decide you must use a video resume to impress an employer, make sure to make it as professional looking as possible. Like a two-page, hard-copy resume, a video resume should be no more than two or three minutes long, and generic enough to interest a range of employers.

- **Fluff**

There is truth in the notion that there can be too much of a good thing. Overuse of any one skill, for example, runs the risk of making a resume appear weighted down by too few skills. It is great to be an expert, or one of the best in at what you do, but look to see if your resume includes related skills and experience. You may the best sheet metal designer, but your natural leadership qualities could also be of interest. Even a slight rebalancing with other skills or interests could increase your exposure to other possibilities.

- **Cover Letters**

Eight out of ten managers report receiving unsolicited email resumes, without a hint of why. When you send a resume by email, through a social network, or over the Internet, be sure, you personalize your correspondence with the manager's name and position. Keep your introduction concise and purposeful. Spending time to create a personalized introduction will improve your chances of having your resume read. A little extra effort will ensure that readers will spend more than the three seconds (yes, three seconds!) it takes to glance over your resume.

- **Retail Resumes in the Hands of Others**

Developing a compelling resume is difficult—very difficult, if taken seriously. It not only requires the use of good English, it has to bring you to life in three dimensions, your personality, interests, and experience. If you feel the task of writing a resume is too daunting, and you can afford assistance, there are commercial resume services, such as resumewriter.com.

☑ Employer Applicant Management Systems (AMS)

Most large companies request applicants submit their resumes and correspondence online or by email. Therefore, if requested to submit a resume as a hard copy, ask the employer how they want the text formatted. **Once the resume is in the employer's Applicant Management System (AMS), the resume can be searched using key words, job titles, acronyms, company names, schools, colleges, universities, dates and locations—just about any criteria.** Obviously, mapping your background to a given open position does not guarantee a "match made in heaven." Nevertheless, mapping will improve chances of your resume being "retrieved."

- **Human Resources Restrictions**

Most corporate policies restrict access to an applicant database to HR specialists, as they are responsible for ensuring fairness, equity, and enforcement of employment policy.

☑ Resumes are a Living Record of Accomplishments

If not kept up to date, resumes can grow stale, overshadowed by more experience, changing interests and personal growth. **Even a modest infusion of action words and crafted language will bring an unconscious resume back to life**. The application of action-packed verbs, electrified work history, and star-studded accomplishments will keep employers on the edge of their seats, asking for more, which is precisely what you want!

CHAPTER NINE
INTERVIEWING

The Art of Job Interviewing

I do not believe that I have had an interview with anybody in twenty-five years in which the person to whom I was talking was not annoyed during the early part of the interview by my asking stupid questions. [Harry Stack Sullivan]

Employment Interviews

On the surface, interviewing for a job should be simple, a process of one person asking questions and another person answering. However, a look below the surface tells a much different story—a much more complex story involving power and trust, control and strategy. In theory, job interviews are an exercise in sharing power. In reality, however, control is often in the hands of the interviewer, often squeezing the applicant's personality, interests, and experience out of the conversation. When conducted properly, good interviewing should satisfy two objectives: a manager's need to fix problems and an applicant's desire to provide solutions. **Review Appendix B, "Twenty Answers to Twenty Tough Job Interview Questions," to get a flavor of the complexity behind common interview questions.**

☑ Inherent Dissonance

Successful interviews depend on minimizing dissonance and maximizing trust, rapport, and credibility. Unfortunately, most applicants have to take the lead to building an interview that minimizes differences and maximizes agreement. Furthermore, interviews are inherently complex by the simple fact that managers and applicants bring their own mix of personalities, interests, and experiences to the meeting. It is no wonder that managers and applicants often talk past, over or under one another

In many ways, interviewing is a natural process, reminiscent of the beginning of language between two cave dwellers. The subject is one of most popular among career counselors and book, authors. **Effective job interviewing is a skill that is learnable and improvable. Furthermore, when used strategically, a job interview can swing control and power your way**. This chapter covers some of the key elements underlying effective job interviews, including:

☑ **Methods**

Employers use interview methods and venues to their advantage. It is their job. Your job, then, is to anticipate and prepare for whatever they throw your way. Realistically, expect most employers to use the most effective and least costly ways of attracting applicants.

- **Telephone**

Aside from a casual interview over a Starbucks coffee, or an intense discussion in the lobby of the Ritz Carlton, or by a pleasant encounter during a transatlantic flight over the Pacific, most **interviews, at least the preliminary ones, will take place by phone, typically with a Human Resources representative.** If contacted by a manager or invited by email to an interview over the phone, be prepared with your updated resume. Have key sections underlined for quick reference. Have the employer's career website open to the job posting, if there is one. In case they ask, have a reference or two handy. However, make sure the employer will not contact any of your references without your permission. This will give you time to brief your references.

- **Face-to-Face**

Whether over the Internet by video conferencing or in the manager's office, the face-to-face interview is the single, most important gateway to employment. Therefore, successful face-to-face interviews depend on one simple principle: the more a manager "sees" what they need in the applicant, the greater the chances of a job offer. Although interview methods and techniques vary with each manager, applicants should employ two strategies: one, focus attention on the job opening, and two, build good face-to-face communications with trust, rapport, and credibility.

- **Job Fairs**

Company Job fairs vary in format, location, and time. **They take place on and off company premises, are open to the public, or conducted by invitation only in order to accommodate**

applicants' work schedules. Large, multi-company job fairs take place in conference centers in hotels or municipal venues. Job fairs are effective because they provide managers immediate access to a self-selected pool of applicants. On the other hand, applicants like job fairs because they expedite face-to-face interviews, with hiring managers and HR specialists. Applicants, who may not have the time or inclination to answer traditional job ads or visit online career sites, will generally take time out of their schedules to meet in person with one or more company managers to explore employment.

One of my employers with a number of US offices decided to expand, so they decided to use job fairs to attract as many applicants as possible, in the shortest amount of time. Each job fair started with a series of Sunday ads, which ran several weeks in a half dozen major newspapers. Management prescreened several hundred applicants before inviting them to the job fair. During the job fair, candidates completed a short form, abbreviated experience profile in order to assign them to a manager in their field of expertise. In some cases, more than one manager interviewed candidates. Those ranked highest on a 5-point scale returned to meet with senior management. The process, which was liked by the applicants, resulted in a number of highly qualified hires.

- **Internet Video**

Occasionally, a company may ask an applicant if they can meet using an Internet video program, such as Skype or Cisco Systems. Video interviewing has been around for some time, but its use is gaining popularity for several reasons. For one, wireless communication is in real-time, and it can save loads of money. All you have to do is compare costs of a video interview to the costs of a round trip airfare between, say California and New York, to make the case. **Video conferencing works particularly well for pre-visit interviews, or for any kind of long distance meeting, for that matter**. If offered the option, be ready with an Internet connection, an inexpensive video camera, or smart phone, and a conferencing service, such as Skype, which is free.

- **Municipal Panels**

The law requires that municipalities, cities, counties, and state agencies use a panel format to interview candidates. Interview panels are usually comprised of up to three or more municipality and industry specialists. **Interview panels are designed to ensure the public that the interview process is fair and consistent.**

- **Technical Presentations**

Academia and research institutions often require their research candidates to make technical presentations as part of the selection process. When I was head of Employment for a major research and development organization, it was common to invite lab candidates to present their findings in a peer-review setting. The format allowed an in-depth evaluation of an applicant's research methods and techniques.

☑ Formats

Most employers use the Traditional question and answer format when conducting job interviews. Other employers sometimes use a more structured approach to interviews by using the Behavioral Interview.

- **Traditional Q & A**

In its simplest form, a traditional interview is a setting where a manager asks questions and an applicant provides answers. The process sounds simple, but the dynamics are complex. In addition to a mix of personalities, interests and experiences of applicants and managers, interviews include elements of power, influence, intimidation, trust, rapport, control, negotiation, credibility, and more. In spite of its complexity and lack of structure, the traditional interview remains the favorite of most employers.

- **Behavioral Interviews**

Unlike the traditional Q & A interview, behavioral interviews base interview questions on a detailed job analysis of the opening. **The analysis dissects a job's duties and responsibilities into criteria proven to link with successful performance**. Applicants describe their experience in terms of a set of performance-based behavioral questions. The method is effective because the questions are job-related. Behavioral interviews have, in the words of an industrial psychologist, "face validity." In other words, besides the side-by-side comparison of an applicant's prior experience with the job to be performed, behavioral interviews rest on the principle of fairness and equity. No hocus-pocus. No oddball tests. Like grades in school, behavioral answers serve as good predictors of future performance. Stated differently, behavior-based questions, like those in the following example for a Program Manager, measure predictability between what has been performed and needs to be performed.

Example: Program Manager

Sample Q: Tell me about your experience as a program manager in charge of both new product development and customer delivery.

Sample Q: Describe your experience managing technical requirements. Please include cost-schedule performance, program assessment, departmental liaison, and customer communications. What average annual budgets were you working with?

☑ Preparation

Most interviews start with a telephone screen by Human Resources. Jumping that hurdle often leads to an invitation to meet face-to-face with a hiring manager. Often stressful, sometimes grueling, but unavoidable, the initial face-to-face meeting is the gateway to further meetings, and potential job offers. Therefore, preparation for a job interview is critical.

- **Necessities**

Provisions for each interview should include a note pad, pen and pencil, names, job titles, telephone numbers, several extra resumes, a calendar, relevant ads or job postings, company information, a sample employment application, and several employment references, much of which can be stored on a smart phone.

- **Date, Time, and Place**

Arrive 5 to 10 minutes early. Allow time for unanticipated traffic delays and difficulties in finding the destination. If available, use a GPS or smart phone to set directions. If time allows, do a dry run a day or two before the meeting. Although Google maps or a GPS can pinpoint an employer's site, an on-site visit, on the other hand, can provide a firsthand look and feel, at ground level. Note location, surroundings, travel time, and your sense of security with the company layout. Some companies are large and intimidating, campus-sized, with multiple buildings and locations.

- **Company Culture**

Before any job interview, be sure to determine as much as you can about the employer's culture. **If you can visit during business hours, collect any sales, product, or services brochures, company** newsletter, annual reports, marketing materials, or online business reports, which may provide clues to a company's culture.

There are vast differences between company cultures, across industries and geographies. In some industries, company culture is obvious. Compare, for example, the computer game industry and the defense industry. Neither culture is better, just distinctly different. Consider, for example, how **different employers recruit employees**. Some companies rely on employee referrals, whereas others concentrate on social networking and others through employment agencies. Similarly, different companies **use different compensation incentives** to reward performance. Some use cash bonuses for performance. **What about reporting relationships? Is the organization flat or hierarchical, with many layers of management? Is the company built on clear lines of authority? Is the company a high-growth, unstructured, start-up?** If organizational structure and strict reporting relationships are important to you, then large, mature corporations may be of interest. Therefore, before accepting or declining an invitation to interview, make sure you have a reasonably good feel for employer's culture. Job postings or want ads will give some hint about company culture, but not much. Apple and General Electric are recognizable, but most companies and their cultures are unknown to the public. If you do not know the company and its culture, start by thinking through your search plan. Do a little research. **Company cultures can be very different from what you would expect from their public image.**

- Appearance

Thoughts of what to wear to an interview can tie a person in knots. Opinion says judgments based on appearance form within the first 10 seconds of a meeting. **Unfortunately, no one has a second chance to make that first impression.** Attire for a sales position interview, for example, is particularly difficult because image is so important.

Whenever possible, visit the employer ahead of time to determine the typical appearance. Are there a lot of suits and ties? Is the look casual, a lot of jackets or short sleeves? I worked for a company where one department accepted sandals, shorts, and beards, whereas other departments required coats and ties. It is hard to tell what the appearance norms are for some companies. When in doubt, default to business casual attire. However, of all the things we wear, expression is the most important.

☑ Interviewing Strategies

- ## Behavior

As an employment manager, when I felt uneasy about an applicant's behavior, or appearance, I would first confirm my impressions. The receptionist often provided the first clues. Applicants who came across as demanding or intimidating were most often sidelined before the interview ever took place. If their manners were inappropriate or disconcerting, we would advise the interviewing manager to skip the interview. **Rude, demanding behavior may strong arm a receptionist, but bad behavior may cost an applicant an opportunity to make a first impression.**

- ## Reduce Tension

Finding someone who is not "stressed out" by a job interview is rare. Nevertheless, you can increase your control, and at the same time reduce the stress of an interview by deflecting attention away from yourself to the interviewer with relevant, appropriately timed, open-ended questions. Early in the interview, you might ask, **"What is your idea of the ideal candidate for this job?"** This simple, benign strategy will give you time to collect your thoughts and take a deep breath. Later in the interview you might ask, **"You have been interviewing for a while, do you have an idea when you might want to make a decision?** Both questions are relevant. Both are deflective. You may have other good questions but want to wait until later in the interview. If so, take notes but stay attentive

- ## Sensitivity to Openers

Complimenting a manager on directions to the interview is a simple, but terrific opener. However, after sharing smiles and niceties, there are some exchanges to avoid. Offering unsolicited comments on personal objects in a manager's office, such as a family photograph, for example, may run the risk of intruding into a manager's personal space. Most managers may not react negatively, but why take the risk? I recall one senior manager complaining that he did not like having to explain the personal history behind a family picture on his desk. The compliment, although offered innocently, came across as too friendly and overly personal, somewhat presumptuous. **There may be a better time for a personal compliments but my recommendation is to keep them to yourself. Instead of gratuitous compliments, concentrate on learning as much as you can about the job.**

- **Determine Ideal Candidate**

The "ideal candidate" question is powerful. The question can work in your favor by giving you the first glimpse into the manager's idea of what he or she feels is most important to the opening. If after you have provided a window into your background, and then ask the question, the interviewer can inflate or minimize the position's job requirements, depending on your qualifications. **The interviewer can use the question as an opportunity to either minimize or inflate the position's job requirements, thereby either diminishing or complementing your qualifications**. Not fair, but strategic use of the question by the interviewer. However, in either case, you come out ahead. Either you know you are included as a candidate or you are out. There is no in between. No wasted time. No questions about what to do next. If given little or no encouragement from the manager, set the meeting aside as a "bust," and move onto the next opportunity. You cannot lose if you stay in control of the process.

- **Confirm Responsibilities**

The Initial interview is often the first chance an applicant has to ask about the opening. At this meeting, applicants are able to clarify a manager's real expectations, not just those in the advertisement. Based on my experience, candidates rarely know the reasons for the opening until the first interview, sometimes not even until the applicant is hired. The reason behind asking for clarification of the responsibilities of the opening is simple—it helps ensure that everyone is on the same page, that there is a clear understanding of the job opening. In addition, asking for clarification demonstrates self-confidence, good listening skills, and recognition of the manager's authority and importance.

- **Use Open-ended Questions**

There are many ways to develop TRC, but one of the best ways is to come to the interview prepared with good open-ended questions, which creates an opportunity to make connections with an interviewer. **Once a degree of rapport is established, continue to probe for more detail on the job and the employer's challenges**. An employer's challenges are unlimited, including: new projects, employee and product turnover, domestic and international competitiveness, information systems, organizational and location issues, real and contemplated acquisitions, deadlines, new and planned products, new services, market contraction and expansion. You name it; you will find it. The point is, problems present opportunities to offer solutions, and the opportunity to demonstrate your credibility.

- **Take Consultant's Approach**

Successful business consultants are great at building trust, rapport, and credibility. They delve into the client's challenges with insightful questions, artfully rephrasing facts, listening closely for opinions, and rephrasing their conclusions. Good consultants are able to time their questions, in order to bring the subject back on track. Good consultants can sniff out information like a thirsty hound dog. At the same time the consultant focuses on the client's issues, they are collecting copious amounts of business information. This process helps create an environment of trust, rapport, and credibility. The point is that applicants can use the same techniques to their advantage. If you can influence the quality of the interview, you can influence its outcome.

- **Be Sensitive to Non-verbal Language**

Non-verbal clues about feelings are evident in most communications, particularly interactions during job interviews. To gauge the quality of the interview, pay attention to the manager's body language, and humor, and your sense of ease and informality. These kinds of signals connote an interest in one's background. They signal trust, rapport, and credibility is developing. If your interview style and communication strategies are working, the interplay between you and the manager will likely lead to more serious two-way discussions. Furthermore, listen carefully to the questions the manager is asking. **Are they reacting favorably to your answers? Are they listening? Have they conveyed a sense of encouragement? Have they asked questions about your future goals? Has the manager asked questions about you want in the way of compensation? What about the interview schedule or the potential for meetings with other companies? Keep your radar active for favorable signals that mean you are on target.**

- **Maintain Professional Stature**

Body language complements attire and appearance. It may seem old school, but, sit up straight and appear attentive. Look at the interviewer. If looking into an interview's eyes is awkward, look above their eyes. Posture and demeanor reflect your confidence and respect for the interviewer.

☑ Trust, Rapport, Credibility (TRC)

- **Trust**

Used in the context of this book, trust is the feeling that **the hiring manager is being honest** about the job's duties and responsibilities, where there are no hidden agendas, no fudging of job requirements, either inflated or minimized. Trust develops when answers to questions are honest, and the manager's assessment of the applicant's qualifications is truthful.

- **Rapport**

The feeling one gets **when an interviewer freely shares their feelings, opinions, and perceptions** with the applicant. An emotional bond develops between people based on mutual liking, and a sense that each other's concerns are understand and shared.

- **Credibility**

An interview defines credibility in the same way accomplishments, contributions, work history, credentials, certification, references, and testimonials define qualifications. A good portion of an interview, in fact, deals with establishing one's credibility. Besides one's resume, there are other ways to establish credibility, including work references, documented experience, special expertise, professional credentials, education, training, and certifications. **Packaged with trust and rapport, credibility triples an applicant's power over the interviewer.**

☑ Wrap-up

- **Final Questions**

It is common for interviewers to apologize for monopolizing the conversation even though they often ask short questions and the applicants give long answers. In any case, to make up for any oversight, or simply to be courteous, most managers will offer to take final questions. Final questions maybe your one and only chance to get lingering issues off your chest. You can hope the manager's offers to ask some final questions, or you can assert yourself by asking for clarification to unanswered questions. Another way to probe a manager's interest is to ask the following question:

I am impressed with the things we discussed. What is the next step in the process? Is there anyone else you can recommend that I meet?

Like the "ideal applicant" question, this one will force a "go, "no go," from the manager. If the manager is unsure of your qualifications, they will likely tell you that there are other candidates to interview. **This may be true, but it is often their use of a delaying strategy**. Express your appreciation for their time, and that you look forward to further discussions. Send a hand-written thank you note a day or so later to close the loop.

- **Final Gestures**

Invariably, even before you offer, most managers will ask for a resume, if for no other reason than curiosity, or as a record of the meeting. A manager may never do anything with your resume, but the request shows a gesture of recognition and support. **If they don't ask for your resume, you might say something like:**

In the event you think of other referrals later, I will leave my resume with you.

☑ Stumbling Blocks

Given an incredible diversity of personalities, interests and experience among applicants and managers, it is no wonder most job interviews turn out to be haphazard. Harry Stack Sullivan, eminent research psychologist, concluded that job interviews, specifically, were an "unpredictable" interweaving of personalities. [Note the word, "unpredictable."] **The fact is, unless managers and applicants share similar personalities, common interests and work experience, the chances of predicting an outcome from any interview may be no better than rolling the dice.**

- **Different Expectations**

Some job interviews leave an applicant wondering, in disbelief, how expectations could be so different. What the applicant thought was an exciting opportunity turns out to be just the opposite, like some real-life, bait and switch. The applicant takes the time to drive a fair distance to interview for a full time job, but learns half way through the meeting that the job is really only part time, for six months. An applicant thinks that personality is key to the job, when, in reality, what the manager really wants is technical expertise. **Whether a manager has a hidden agenda, or has misplaced priorities, different expectations can ruin a day**. My advice is simple: if you have any doubts about the job and its responsibilities, check again with the manager or contact HR. No one can eliminate different expectations, but one can minimize the surprise and disappointment.

- **Employment Gaps**

Actively looking for new employment with more than a six-month gap, may tarnish a perfect resume. Nevertheless, one way to clear the air is to call attention to the gap before the interviewer raises the issue. Questions about periods of brief unemployment may not seem relevant to you, but may *not* be trivial to the interviewer. Beyond a simple, "looking for another position," is prepared to explain any gaps in employment. You may have a number of reasons, including concentrating on looking for work, and how the time off has provided a chance to reassess your skills and career goals. ***"Although my employment search has not paid off yet, I am sill enthused about joining a company who needs good people motivated to work again."*** Whatever your efforts, be ready with an answer. Filling in any employment Q & A gaps will help confirm the applicant's credibility. The net result will be a more complete employment history in the eyes and ears of the employer.

- **"Job Hopper"**

The idea of excessive jobs is relative. What I or any other manager might consider excessive may not be excessive to you. The same goes for the label, "job hopper." However, if you worry that you suffer from the job hopper label, there may be legitimate reasons you can use to explain the situation. The need to provide childcare or attend classes may only fit for temporary jobs. Alternatively, working in an industry suffering cutbacks and outsourcing may force one into a number of shorter-term jobs. Whatever the reason, and there are many as a result of the great recession, approach the issue with an upbeat, plausible explanation. Remember, most people change jobs out of necessity, and with good reasons. On the other hand, if for some reason, you find yourself changing jobs due to an unclear career path, you may want to look to counseling resources and support to help determine your inner goals.

- **Defensive Reactions**

It is natural to be defensive when badgered by an argumentative interviewer. Nevertheless, try not to take this kind of interviewing style personally. It has nothing to do with you. This interviewing style may be just that, a style intended to test an applicant's reaction to criticism. When you feel yourself reacting defensively, try countering the reaction by reminding yourself of your core convictions. In spite of what someone else says, you know you are a worthy applicant for any employer. **Remember, no matter how much an interviewer may try to demean, push buttons, or impugn your worthiness, stand by your core Resilience, be they the knowledge that you are fair and honest, ethical in your dealings with others, are experienced and competent, or empathetic towards those in need.** Whatever core Resilience you conjure up, they will offset defensive reactions.

- **Poorly Timed Questions**

A good sense of timing can mean the difference between failure and success. Timing is universally important, particularly during an employment interview. Bad timing cannot only foul up a car's engine; it can gum up an interview. **Inadvertently or deliberately interjecting a question about promotional schedules during a manager's explanation on job duties will jam a wedge into a manager's thought process.** A question, out of left field has the same effect as being rear-ended. A zinger out of now where, out of context will mangle any chance of having a successful interview.

- **Inappropriate Questions**

Some questions are simply inappropriate, asked out of context, at the wrong time, by innuendo, or simply presumption. In my experience, I have seen more interviews flattened by inappropriate questions than by lack of qualifications.

What does your company do? [Why appear unprepared?]

Are you going to do a background check? [Are you concealing something illegal?]

When will I be eligible for a raise? [Question is presumptive. Restate the question with the following: When are employees eligible for a performance review and a raise in pay?]

Do you have any other jobs available? [Is the manager responsible for finding your next job?]

What is your policy on drugs and smoking? [Why ask unless you have something to hide?]

Similarity, there is no need to volunteer your medical history. **However, if an employer asks if you have a condition that might affect your ability to perform the job, particularly one that requires physical strength, or lifting and reaching, answer honestly.** If you do have a physical condition, employers have an obligation to consider an accommodation, such wheelchair access, or modification to shelving height. However, many medical conditions do not automatically require an employer accommodation. It often depends on how expensive or unreasonable an accommodation might be. The issue is for Human Resources to sort out.

- **Answer Overload**

Answering a manager's questions with too much information can swamp an interview. However, you can keep your boat afloat by applying brevity. Brevity means using words economically. As a communications skill, it requires good listening and the ability to collect and process questions into concise answers. **Brevity creates an image of confidence, organization, and control, qualities most managers appreciate in busy work environments**. Granted, answering interview questions concisely is not easy, especially under stress. It is natural to ramble occasionally. **However, the inclination to say more, in order to share more, in order to convince more, in hopes of receiving more, is, frankly, a losing strategy**. You can be brief, and to the point, without sacrificing substance. When preparing for your next interview, be sure to break the job description into its key criteria. Next, draft brief, concise responses to mock questions. We often say more than is needed during an interview hoping the interviewer will reciprocate with positive comments on our qualifications. **We search for confirmation of our talents even if we know the job is a poor fit. We listen for gratuitous compliments, or a simple expression of approval: a smile, a nod, an invitation to meet again, any sign of approval that we have what it takes to be a great employee. Unfortunately, the strategy does not work**. It's better to concentrate on forging a balanced, two-way conversation, than to look for compliments. **Too much talking by the applicant and too little interviewing by the manager will undercut the value of an interview**. Brevity is not only the key to good interviews, it will help keep your interviewer awake and alert during the process.

- **Personal Bias**

Some supervisory styles leave an indelible image in one's memory, mostly good, the kind that encourages growth and development and open communication, whereas others squash initiative, constantly criticizes performance and micro-manage. **Strong preferences, for or against a particular management style can cloud an interview.** It is better to downplay pre-conceived manager preferences and, instead, concentrate on the interviewer's treatment of you and consideration of your qualifications. **Nevertheless, if asked by a manager to describe the management style you prefer, keep your answers upbeat and positive, emphasizing how you know the importance of supporting management and the importance that recognition, mutual**

support, and self-sufficiency play in creating a successful team. Most managers do their best to be thoughtful and fair with their employees, but sometimes their interview style verges on the terrible.

☑ **Employer Strategies: Applicant Tactics**

- **Professional: Mutual sharing of information and goals**

Good interviewers make sure they know what they are looking for in an applicant. They review their qualifications, and formulate job-centered questions. During the interview, good interviewers ask clear, concise questions, giving the applicant time to respond. They clarify answers, making sure they understand any nuances. They are sensitive to the stress of an interview and the pressure an applicant may feel. They believe in making the experience as comfortable as possible. Questions are germane to the applicant's qualifications. **Luckily, good interviewers are the norm, not the exception.**

However, there are the exceptions—and they are big ones. It is rare, but some managers use questionable or unethical interview techniques. We have all met a few along the way. Granted interviewing applicants is tough and should be taken seriously by a manager.

- **Biased: Concentrate on contributions and job requirements**

Stereotyping others before or during an interview is fraught with problems, some of them illegal. **Although there are many forms of stereotyping, from race to sex, none is more pervasive than age.** It is clear that some interviewers suffer from vision defects. They fail to see in front of them the many benefits the older, more experienced worker can bring to a job.

There is no substitute for actual "shirts sleeve, hard-knocks" experience. The more experienced engineer, for example, will use experience and intuition to his or her advantage, thereby reducing trial and error, saving valuable financial and human resources. First, instead of getting an expensive facelift, or out-and-out lying, **concentrate on situations where you used creativity to solve complex problems. The second strategy is to push the interview to explain in detail their challenges, whether technical, financial or-personnel. This strategy will take some skill, but will help shift attention toward the reason for the opening, and toward your qualifications.**

- **Skeptic: Concentrate on transferable skills equivalent goals**

Skeptics are less tyrannical, but more cynical. However, the effects are the same; an applicant's experience is shortchanged. **The skeptic discounts qualifications on the first reading of a resume, rejecting the notion that qualifications are transferrable.** The skeptic's interview comes down hard on applicants trying to transition from the one industry to another, particularly for those trying to move from the public sector to private industry. However, there are ways to overcome the skeptic's reluctance. **The first and most important strategy to overcoming the skeptic's reluctance is knowledge.** Understanding the differences and similarities between industry sectors is tantamount to convincing a manager that most qualifications are transferrable between industries. Case in point: public vs. private sector. **The following table illustrates the different descriptions for common industries features, such as method of hiring and reporting relationships.** Awareness of differences and similarities between industries will help counter the skeptic's reluctance to accept your qualifications.

Responsibility	PUBLIC Sector	PRIVATE Sector
Income	Taxes	Investors/Profits
Performance	Budget Driven	Cost Driven
Hire Method	Competitive Exams/Panels	Manager
Size	Large/Complex	Small/Specialized
Organizational Design	Bureaucratic	Flat, Bureaucratic/Mixed
Communication Flow	Top-Down	Lateral/Decentralized
Decision Process	Cautious/Protracted	Decisive/"Bottom line"
Reporting Relationships	Defined	Amorphous/Multiple
Job Descriptions	Defined /Responsibilities	Situational, Project, Process
Manager Tenure	Tenured	At will

- **The Inexperienced: Emphasize duties, responsibilities and expectations**

Like the other thorny interviews, sometimes you do encounter an inexperienced interviewer. It is very difficult to prepare for an interviewer who uses an open-ended, unstructured approach; the kind of interview who is appears confused and muddled. They are confused about the job, about which the applicant is seen next, or about why they have been asked to conduct an interview. **Your strategy with the incompetent interviewer is to stay focused on the job opening. If they don't seem to know, remind them about the nature of the job, and about specific duties and responsibilities, reporting relationships, and projects and challenges. It may not help much, but your strategy will keep the train of thought and flow of questions from completely flying off the rails.**

☑ Role-playing

Role-playing is often used as a means of developing insight and skill. I used the approach with groups I worked with. I would typically start the role-playing by asking each client to describe how he or she obtained his or her last job. I asked questions like how the manager conducted the job interview, or how they found their last job. We discussed their initial interactions with the company, the receptionist, and the human resources representative. We explored their evaluation of the job interview and the kinds of questions asked. Most often, we spent time telling about their experience with those who decided on the hire. Although we all laughed at the opportunity to embellish the more outlandish experiences, some of which could serve as episodes on the TV series *The Office*, once we had our fun, everyone role-played the manager, and then switched roles, to play the applicant. **A chance to role-play a manager provided a different perspective, one from the other side of the desk. We saw the humor in the serious, which helped minimize failure and disappointment.** We shared observations, opinions, and experience, by emphasizing gentle, but insightful feedback from others in the group. **The exercises gave everyone the chance to practice different communication strategies, which provided insight into the interview process.** Practicing the art of interviewing proved valuable to most. Therefore, jump, run or demand the chance to practice the art of interviewing, whenever you have the chance.

- **Room for Improvement**

The beauty of interviewing skills, any skill for that matter, is that they can always improve. Although not innate, job interviewing is simply another form of communication, which one can improve. That means learning to take an active, assertive role in the interview process, controlling, or at least modulating, the two-way exchange between you and the interviewer. The goal is to convey the strength of your personality, your interests, and your experience. The process begins right from the start, right from the opening dialogue with the manager.

- **Practice makes perfect**

Professional athletes live the adage that practice makes perfect. For any sport, skating, soccer, hockey, or gymnastics, there is no substitute for practice, perseverance, and failure. Practice, by its very nature, encourages mistakes, and failures. Honing performance is sometimes rocky. In spite of any downside, practice will increase one's self-confidence and self-esteem.

CHAPTER TEN

NEGOTIATING

Strategic Use of Power

Choose a job you love, and you will never have to work a day in your life. [Confucius]

Negotiating the Job Offer

As the universal means of arriving at agreement, negotiating is unsurpassed. Because negotiating is mostly an art, one can shift one's advantage from side to side, in favor of one or the other. Negotiations are subjective, like viewing a painting where reaction is in the eye of the beholder. Whether negotiating a tug of war between a mom and obstinate toddler, between two ambassadors brokering a nuclear arms agreement, or a hiring manager and candidate, negotiations serve the means of arriving at agreement. Negotiations define human dialogue between political leaders, neighbors over land rights, mothers and children, and between employers and candidates. No matter what the circumstance, negotiating is a skill worth developing, particularly when it comes to job offers.

Negotiations echo like sounds in a tennis match, each player looking to score more points, or acquire advantage. As a special form of dialogue, **negotiating has the power to move candidates and managers closer to mutual agreement on pay and benefits, responsibilities, and reporting relationships.** Negotiating job offers span the emotional gamut. They can be intimidating or harmonious, even joyous; it all depends on how each party feels about the ground they have surveyed and acquired. In any event, effective negotiating requires smart, educated compromise; the kind of compromise that balances the demand for perfection.

As your strategies begin to improve the power to influence others, one's perseverance and commitment begin to confirm what has been known—that earlier decisions, plans, and commitments have taken hold, like the roots of a great redwood tree. Time and effort merge with a sense of confidence and optimism that job offers are waiting in the wings to take stage. The question is, will you be prepared to negotiate an offer?

☑ Interviews—Start, During, and Wrap-up, Preparation

Negotiating job offers mixes the art of persuasion with the science of contracts, mostly in favor of the employer. Nevertheless, when an offer hits your doorstep there are communications strategies that will shift negotiations your way. As before any sports event, competitors make sure they are prepared, mentally and physically to negotiate for their side. Preparing to negotiate or bargain for what you want should include the following:

- **Rule 1: Conduct Comprehensive Research**

Before you head off into the hinterlands, take time to research industries, occupations, and jobs of interest. For example, if you target a job market in the greater Dallas Texas area for computer manufacturing, research prevailing pay levels for your skills and talents. It is a good idea to research as many specifics as you can, including employers, industry types, and levels of openings. Determine the need for temporary workers, or contract employees, and regular full-time positions. Scour local newspapers for articles on business growth, plant expansion, and more. Contact the local Chamber of Commerce for news releases and employer lists. Check with the local Department of Employment. Swing the advantage your way: the more specific your information, the better your negotiating power.

- **Rule 2: Know Your Priorities**

A simple suggestion, but this one helps organize your priorities: start with three columns, the first marked "needs," and the other two marked, "wants" and "interests." Consider column one, "needs", as must haves, like your baseline salary. The second column, "wants" are parts of offer you would like to get, such as a parking stall. These you can trade for other items of an offer. Finally, the third column, marked, "interests," are "trial balloons" that are intended to test a manager's willingness to negotiate outside the ordinary employment conditions. Interests are nice to have, like an inflated job title, but not critical to the offer.

- **Rule 3: Know the Employer's Priorities**

Information means advantage. Knowing what employers need in the way of solutions puts the applicant in a great position. Is the employer ramping up production or simply expanding to accommodate growth? Are they new to the area? Is the opening the result of a new contract? Has overseas manufacturing failed to meet demand in the US? Is there a huge push to change computer systems?

An employer's priorities and problems keep managers up at night. Once you have a good idea what challenges the manager is wrestling with, focus on her or his priorities. Determine the kinds of value you can bring to the show. This strategy will endure you when it comes to negotiating your position in the hearts and minds of the employer.

- **Rule 4: Know What You Need in Pay and Benefits**

Enter negotiations with a clear sense of where you stand on pay and benefits, and your willingness to bargain. A simple but practical approach is to set two levels of pay, the first roughly ten percent above what you would accept, and the second ten percent lower than what you would accept. Consider the first level, "sweet," and the second, "sour." Somewhere in between would be your target pay. Depending on additional information you may receive, be prepared to adjust your target range. Nevertheless, whatever strategy you chose, be prepared to negotiate before the first job offer catches you flatfooted. The sheer excitement of receiving an offer, if unemployed for some time, can easily diminish one's ability to negotiate for what one may want or need.

- **Rule 5: Use Your Behavioral Strengths to Advantage**

Occupational experience may be your strongest negotiating chip, but don't forget the power your personality can have on the negotiating process. Personality may not be the cake, but it can certainly be the frosting.

If packaged properly, under the right circumstances, the strength of one's personality can tilt the negotiating advantage your way. Why? Because the strength of one's personality can serve to offset the lack of specific work experience. Therefore, before you discount the notion that a warm smile, a friendly handshake, or that good listening skills have nothing to do with success, think again. In my experience, a winning, warm personality has often meant the difference between an offer and rejection.

☑ **Negotiating Strategies**

Most managers develop negotiating strategies and techniques. For example, some managers will help a candidate decide on pay and benefits, and tradeoffs, whereas other managers will stand firm, like statues, unyielding and uncompromising, pressuring the candidate into a take-it-or—leave-it-posture. Some managers are masters at extracting agreements, whereas others turn negotiations over to Human Resources. No matter the negotiating style or negotiator, your strategy is to remain focused on the features of the offer that include what you want and the kinds of tradeoffs that you can negotiate for to improve your position.

- **Be the First to Determine Ideal Salary for the Job**

Before the employer has a chance to determine your ideal salary, get to their position first. First is better than second. Whenever a hint of salary is raised during the discussion, take the lead to establish the manager's position on salary by asking a simple, straightforward question: *What is your ideal salary for this position?* They may be cagey on this question because they know their answer will put you in a better position to help you determine your next move.

If the manager states the ideal salary for the job to be ten percent above your ideal pay, your decision may be a slam-dunk. On the other hand, if the employer offers a salary ten percent below your ideal, you may want to consider negotiating. Of course, you could also ask if their ideal salary is within the job's compensation range. An offer low in the range may mean potential salary growth. If high in the range, the offer could mean nominal growth, or potential for promotion into the next higher classification. In any event, with nothing to lose, you can always counter with what you feel is acceptable. If your counter offer is rejected, exit and move onto the next opportunity.

- **Trade Your Position on Pay for More Information on the Job**

Why delay answering questions about pay or salary? First, because negotiating one's position strengthens, the more one knows about a job's true requirements and responsibilities, the better. Secondly, because pay is often the means of screening a candidate, most managers will try to start negotiations by probing for salary expectations. On the other hand, you want to hold back on your salary needs until you are comfortable with the job and its responsibilities, a manager will probably still push to find out what you want in the way of pay. Managers will try to get a sense early in the interview of where you stand on salary. They may work their questions around the pay issue or go directly to the subject with something like: **What kind of a salary are you looking for?**

The question sounds innocuous, innocent enough; straightforward, simple, and seemingly easy to answer, however, one person's strategy is another person's opportunity. One way around the employer's question is to answer with something like:

Thanks for asking. I am currently making $x per year, not counting other company benefits [including performance bonus, extra vacation, company stock match, etc.]. As you know, at this point in my career, I am looking for more responsibility and growth. [This type of answer places the ball back in the applicant's court].

When discussing compensation, many applicants fear appearing too "expensive." If you are one of these, and the interview migrates toward pay or salary, balance your response about your pay history with more information about responsibilities and challenges. Consultants, for example, receive compensation according to their experience and expertise. Greater pay is generally commensurate with greater responsibilities.

- **Never Give Away a Chance to Trade**

In other words, never give up something without getting something in return. Unless you are a member of a union or professional organization, where others handle negotiations, there is frequently some room during offer negotiations for give and take. For example, if the manager counters your push for salary, ask instead for an extra week of vacation, or a sign-on bonus, or a performance bonus. If the manager rejects your counter offers, do not give up. Try other tradeoffs. If not a hire-on bonus, ask, instead, for a trip to Tahiti. Whatever tradeoffs you have in mind, have a plan of what you want and what you will trade. As with the game of chess, use pay, benefits and work conditions as pawns to trade. Remain flexible, listen carefully, stay cool under pressure, and downplay absolute pay expectations.

- **Use Silence to Send a Loud Message**

Used sparingly silence is golden during negotiations. If a manager tries to negotiate a lower salary, hold your reaction, stand silent. The delay will signal its own message. A slight shrug of the shoulders or a slow, head movement will signal displeasure. Break the tension with a counter offer or a trade-off. The "who blinks first" strategy may be a bit stressful, but the results may be worth the momentary tension.

- **Leverage Release of Employment References**

One of the first signs an offer may be in the works is a manager's request for employment references. This is a good sign, but release of your references should not be free. Be sure to make release of any references contingent on an employer's sincere interest in your background, particularly an interest in making you an offer. In other words, do not release your employment references until you are confident the employer is serious. Once you have a clearer picture of the offer, you are now in a better position to brief your references, before the employer catches them by surprise.

Catching a reference by surprise may cause her or him to hesitate, possibly creating an impression they are hiding negative information. You can maintain advantage by reminding your references of your experience, notable performance, special achievements, and any exceptional contributions. **Tell your references why the job is important to you, be it growth, additional training, or another step to a grander plan and more responsibility.** Discuss the job being offered, including basic responsibilities, and reporting relationships. This strategy can turn a simple request for references into a home run strategy.

☑ **Employer Strategies**

How managers negotiate job offers varies from employer to employer, industry to industry, and from occupational field to occupational field. In some companies, managers have the sole authority to negotiate virtually any salary they wish, whereas, in other companies, upper management micromanages every step of the offer process. Negotiations with executive candidates, for example, are handled differently from those with entry-level candidates. Offers to executives, for instance, are often negotiated between the executive's agent, such as a recruiter, and the company's President or the Board of Director's Compensation Committee. Whereas, offers to non-management applicants are made directly to the candidate and are often on a take it or leave it basis. However, there are always some elements of an offer that can be negotiated, no matter how small.

- **Testing the Applicant's Acceptance**

When a manager asks you if the offer salary is acceptable, there are many ways to answer, including a simple nod, but you could, instead, respond with something like:

The offer sounds good. However, as a matter of curiosity, where does it fit within the job's salary range? [Strategic use of follow-up questions can pass the advantage back into your court.]

☑ Non-Cash Benefits

Recruiting new hires and holding onto current staff is a balancing act in perpetual motion. Beyond pay, other employer benefits, such as health coverage, are an important company magnet. Those in the public sector are often attracted by better than average non-cash benefits, such as health, vacation, sick leave, life insurance, long-term disability, and better than average, retirement plans. An employer's contributions to employee benefits or a retirement match can mean an additional 25 to 40 percent in addition to base salary. Companies and municipalities that offer employer paid health plans, for example, are at a distinct recruiting advantage.

Non-cash benefits, such as health insurance tend to be similar from company to company, within the same industry, across the US. However, they can vary substantially, depending on employee demographics, such as age, marital status, and family size. Therefore, non-cash benefits should be a major consideration in accepting or rejecting a job offer.

☑ Competing Offers

It may seem far-fetched, but some applicants actually do receive more than one job offer, not counting their employer's appeal to stay. Gradually, tenacious applicants begin to see the fruits of their labor, in the shape of competing offers. Multiple offers are wonderful for the ego, but come with a basket full of stress and conflict. **Negotiating more than one employment offer requires serious tact, discipline, and courage, which of course, is more art than science.**

• **Juggling More Than One Offer**

If you are one of the lucky ones with more than one offer, take time to analyze the pluses and minuses of each. Ask yourself if the offers are competitive in terms of pay and benefits. Are the responsibilities roughly comparable? How do you feel about the potential managers? Are you comfortable with their management styles? What about potential colleagues? Did you have a chance to meet any of them? What chances are there to receive training and develop new skills? If you have to commute, how much will it cost in time and money? What about work schedules and business travel? Do you have to relocate? **List the pluses and minuses to accepting any one of the offers. Consider them all before making your decision.**

It is a little tricky, but you may have to hold one company at bay while negotiating with another. This strategy is tricky and can be nerve-racking. The expression, *A bird in the hand is worth two in the bush,* was invented for just this kind of dilemma. If you decide to proceed, there are several strategies from which to choose.

Explain that you do not want to miss an excellent opportunity, but that another company is pushing you for an answer.

Apologize, but explain that you do not want to make any decisions without considering another company's offer first.

Be careful not to risk irritation. Keep the dialogue open by making appear you are still very interested in their offer.

☑ Final Decisions

When you have considered all the options, is it time to make the final decision on the job offer.

- **Special Features of an Offer**

When you receive an offer, by email, phone, letter, or by certified mail, take a few days to make sure it reflects your understanding. Be clear about any special provisions for unforeseen situations, such as a reduction in force or a dramatic change in business conditions.

- **Sign-on Bonuses**

Some employers will offer a "sign-on" bonus to entice acceptance. Sign-on or hire bonuses are used for a couple of reasons. For one, sign-on bonuses often tip the applicants decision in favor of the employer. Secondly, sign-on bonuses are a way to reduce potential salary inequities between new employees and existing employees. Existing employees' salaries often drift below market competition, therefore, making new offers look too high unless they are offset with a sign-on bonus. If the employer offers a sign-on bonus, look carefully at the method of taxation. Will the employer "gross up" the hire-on bonus to offset additional taxes? Does the employer have available the services of a tax accountant? Make sure that special vacation provisions are accurate, particularly if they exceed company policy.

- **Confirm Final Decision**

When considering the impact a job offer makes, be sure to remind yourself to consider that the decision that will affect your near and long-term career objectives. Before making a final decision, test the offer against one or more of the following questions:

Will rejecting an offer that does not meet my goals be better than waiting for an unknown offer in the future?

Should I accept this offer just to gain employment?

Should I alter my original goals in favor of new ones?

Am I basing my decision on the potential this offer provides?

Do the risks involved in this offer, such as relocation or career change, outweigh pay and benefits?

☑ Offer in Writing

Not quite a marriage prenuptial, but getting an offer in writing is simply a good business practice. Offers of employment that include relocations, overseas benefits or hazardous duty premiums, for example; and hire-on or performance bonuses, for instance, stock grants, options, or other special provisions, such as immigration assistance, should be put in writing. Some provisions are complex and may be very important. Written contracts are the backbone of business. In fact, managers know the value of agreements and contracts. **More often than not, managers will respect an applicant's request to have an offer in writing.** Ask for the offer in writing with something like the following Rules:

May I have the offer in writing? I want to be sure I understand the conditions and provisions discussed during our conversations.

When the honeymoon is over, it is easy to forget the promises made during the romance. If you do not receive a confirming offer letter, ask for one. Memory is not as permanent as the written word.

- **Blinded by Euphoria**

A job offer can be exhilarating, exuberating, mystical, or overwhelming. Like winning the lotto, a Job offer validates self-worth. It affirms hard work, good planning, and perseverance. Visions of the future may look so bright they can temporally blind good judgment. An employment offer may mean the difference between living a bad dream and a bright future. Blinded by euphoria is like a deer in the headlights, there is a powerful temptation for some to accept any offer, whatever its worth.

- **Indecision**

Suppose you have aced the last two interviews, and your sense of confidence is frankly, soaring. You are beginning to feel, unabashedly, invincible. Criticisms? No big deal. A critical remark? Just another lame—brained opinion? Yet, within the reaches of your consciousness, deep down, in a corner, lie the nagging, tugging, irksome seeds of doubt. Being pressed to accept an offer, but pulled at the same time by indecision and doubt will sow fields of conflict.

Negotiating with one's self pushes one to wait until the bell counts down to round ten, beckoning one to stay and fight for that next better offer, the one that offers more security, more money, and more opportunity. The dilemma is like the classic TV quiz show, "Let's Make a Deal," where the contestant is asked to go for door number one, which may contain a better prize, or accept the prize in hand. In real life, decisions like these are common. **You can weigh the pros and cons, repeatedly, but, at some time, you have to make a decision, even if it is to walk away from the negotiating table.**

- **Stretching Indecision to the breaking point**

Do not stretch your decision too far. Most employers will ask for a decision within a week or two, at the outside. Therefore, be careful not to push the envelope. If your request is for more than two weeks to make a decision, the manager may view the delay more a ploy to leverage other offers. Even in those cases where the answer is an obvious "yes," ask for a day or two to think about it. However, reinforce your enthusiasm by indicating:

The offer looks great, but I would like a little more time before making a final decision.

Delaying your decision to accept or reject an offer provides an opportunity to explore in more detail incidental goodies, such as a laptop, tablet, or smart phone. Ask about policies, such as education and training, or cost reimbursements. If the job requires relocation, ask what expenses are covered. The time between the decision to accept or reject is a great time to negotiate improved terms and conditions. The chances of successfully bargaining on the offer are greater than not.

☑ Decision Time

Armed with sufficient information, such as duties, responsibilities, and expectations, it is time to confront the offer with a decision to either accept or decline. Stop for a moment and ask, if you feel pushed to make a decision. Do you get the sense the manager is inflexible? In other words, it is a take it or leave it proposition? Are they asking what it will take to "extract" an acceptance? You can decide yes or no.

- **Accepting an Offer**

Accepting a job offer can be a joyous moment. Offers typically come by phone, followed by a hard copy delivered by a mail service, such as FedEx, with a return receipt requested. A "yes" seals the deal.

☑ Confirmation of Your Value

When the offer does arrive, remember it came because you did a great job of communicating the strength of your personality, your interest in the employer's work and mission, your solid history of experience, and your record of accomplishments. Be sure to use good judgment when negotiating the offer, so that you and the manager will both come away **with a win-win situation.** Regardless of the eventual outcome, the job offer is your reward for all your hard work, so congratulate yourself and take time to enjoy the fruits of your labor!

- **Rejecting the Offer**

It happens. The offer is great, but not great enough. You could take a hint from Paul Simon's 1975 song hit, *50 Ways to Leave Your Lover,* but there are easier and less painful ways to decline an employer's offer of employment. It can be as simple as a telephone call or an email. However, before saying no to an offer, make sure to listen carefully to an employer's expectations. Is the offer open to further discussions? Can the offer be sweetened? The reason or reasons for rejecting an offer range from simple (salary too low) to complex (uneasy with manager's communication style, to unsure about industry problems). In any event, if you decide to decline an offer you can do it with something like:

Thanks very much for the generous offer, but after a good deal of thought, I have decided to continue my search for a position that offers a little more responsibility. On the other hand, the employer may retract the offer. The worst of the worst.

[Employer's Retraction]

Retracting an offer is not the kind of strategy an employer wants to use. The pain travels both ways. As employment and hiring manager, I have felt the gut-wrenching disappointment of a candidate withdrawing their acceptance, in the same way that I have seen what happens when a company retracts their offer. Retractions are not the fault of the candidate or the hiring manager. There is no salve for the pain and disappointment a job offer retraction can cause. However, if it ever happens to you, my advice is to accept the retraction with as much maturity as possible, as hurtful as it might be. Stay in contact with the manager. I can assure you, in my experience, the managers I worked with were very willing to help offset a candidate's distress, partly to alleviate their own sense of guilt.

References

Aspinwall, L.G., and S.E. Taylor. (1992). Modeling Cognitive Adaptation: A Longitudinal Investigation of the Impact of Individual Differences and Coping with College Adjustment and Performance. *Journal of Personality and Psychology. 63, 6, 989-1003.*

Bassett, G. (1965). *Practical Interviewing.* New York: American Management Association, Haddon Craftsmen, Inc., Publisher.

Beatty, Richard H. (1989). *The Perfect Cover Letter.* New York: John Wiley & Sons.

Berkowitz, L. (Ed). ((1988*). Advances in experimental social psychology. Vol. 21, pp. 1-361 ISBN: 978-0-12-015221-6*

Blau, Peter. (1956*). Bureaucracy in Modern Society.* New York: Random House.

Bolger N, Zuckerman A. (1995). A framework for studying personality in the stress process. *Journal of Personality & Social Psychology. 69(5), 890-902.* [PubMed].

Bois, J. (1957). *Explorations in Awareness.* New York: Harper & Brothers, Publishers.

Bradford, D., Cohn, A. (1984). *Managing for Excellence.* New York: John Wiley and Sons.

Bradford, D., Gibb, J., and Benne, K. (1964). *T-Group Theory and Laboratory Method.* New York: John Wiley and Sons.

Bridges, William. (*1994). Job Shift.* Reading, MA: Addison-Wesley.

Burley-Allen, M. (1982). *Listening, the Forgotten Skill.* New York: John Wiley and Sons.

Career Development: (Adopted March 16, 1993). Revised 2003. *A Policy Statement of the National Career Development Association Board of Directors.*

Christensen A.J, Ehlers S.L, Wiebe J.S, Moran P.J, Raichle, K., Ferneyhough, K., Lawton, W.J. (2002). Patient personality and mortality: A 4-year prospective examination of chronic renal insufficiency. *Health Psychology; 21, 315-320.* [PubMed].

Cohen, G. L., Aronson, J, Steele, C. M. (2000). When beliefs yield to evidence: Reducing biased evaluation by affirming the self. *Personality and Social Psychology Bulletin, 26, 1151-1164.*

Correll, J., Spencer, S. J., Zanna, M. P. (2004). An affirmed self and an open mind: Self-affirmation and sensitivity to argument strength. *Journal of Experimental Social Psychology, 40, 350-356.*

Corwen, L. (1980). *Get the Job You Want.* Toronto, Canada: Coles Publishing Co. Ltd.

Creswell, J. D., Welch, W., Taylor, S. E., Sherman, D. K., Gruenewald, T., & Mann, T. (2005). Affirmation of personal values buffers neuroendocrine and psychological stress responses. *Psychological Science, 16, 846-851.*

Cronback, Lee J. (1960). *Essentials of Psychological Testing.* New York: Harper & Brothers, Publishers.

Digman, J.M. (1990). Personality Structure, Emergence of the Five-Factor Model. *Annual Review of Psychology*, Palo Alto, CA.

Elder, G.H. (1999) Children of the great depression. Social change in life experience. 25. Anniversary print, Boulder: Westview Press Farr, J., (1991).

Fleishman, E. (1961). *Studies in Personnel and Industrial Psychology.* Homewood, IL: The Dorsey Press, Inc.

Friedman HS. (1991-2000). *Self-Healing Personality: Why Some People Achieve Health and Others Succumb to Illness.* New York: Holt.

Friedman HS, Silver RC, editors. (2007). Personality, disease, and self-healing. *Foundations of Health Psychology.* NY: Oxford University Press. 172-199.

Friedman HS., Tucker JS., Schwartz JE, Tomlinson-Keasey C, Martin LR., Wingard DL., Criqui MH. (1995) Psychosocial and behavioral predictors of longevity: The aging and death of Termites. *American Psychologist.* 50:69-78. [PubMed].

Gilbert, D. T., Pinel, E. C., Wilson, T. D., Blumberg, S. J., & Wheatley, T. P. (1998). Immune neglect: A source of durability bias in affective forecasting. *Journal of Personality and Social Psychology.* 75, 617-638.

Goffman, Erving.(1959). *The Presentation of Self in Everyday Life.* Doubleday: Garden City, NY:

Goodwin RG, Friedman HS. (2006). Health status and the Five Factor personality traits in a nationally representative sample. *Journal of Health Psychology.* 11, 643-654. [PubMed].

Hahn, H, and Stout, R. (1994). *The Internet Yellow Pages,* New York: Osborne McGraw-Hill.

Haldane, B. (1981). *Career Satisfaction and Success.* New York: AMECON.

Hall, Calvin S., Lindzey, Gardner. (1962). *Theories of Personality.* New York: John Wiley, and Sons, Inc.

Hayakawa, S. I. (1940). *Language in Thought and Action.* New York: Harcourt, Brace and Company.

Herr, E.L., & Cramer, S. H. (1996). Career guidance and counseling through the lifespan: Systematic approaches. New York: Harper Collins.

Holland, John L. (1997). *Making Vocational Choices-3nd Edition.* Odessa, FL: Psychological Assessment Resources.

Holland John L. (1992). *Making Vocational Choices,* Third edition, *A Theory of Vocational Personalities and Work Environments.* Odessa, FL: Psychological Assessment Resources.

Holland, John L., Fritzsche, B.A., Powell, A.B. (1994). *The Self-Directed Search Technical Manual.* Odessa, FL: Psychological Assessment Resources.

Holland John L., Gottfredson, G. E. (1992). Studies of the hexagonal model: evaluation or the perils of stalking the perfect hexagon. *Journal of Vocational Behavior,* 40, 158-170.

Holland, John L., and Nicholas, R.C. (1964). Explorations of a theory of vocational choice: III. A longitudinal study of change in major field of study. *Personnel and Guidance Journal,* 43, 235-42.

Hollander, Dory. (1991). *The Doom Loop.,* New York: Viking Penguin Group.

Howard, Ann, Editor, (1995). *The Changing Nature of Work.* San Francisco, CA: Jossey-Bass Publishers. Insel, Paul M., Roth, Walton T. (1991). *Core Concepts in Health.* Mountain View, CA: Mayfield Publishing Company.

Johnson, Steven. (2010). *Where Good Ideas Come From.* New York: Riverhead Books.

Judge, T.A., Ilies, R. (2002). Relationship of personality to performance motivation: A meta-analytic review. *Journal of Applied Psychology.* 87(4), 797-807. [PubMed].

Kaumeyer, R. (1979). *Planning and Using Skills Inventory Systems.* New York: Van Nostrand Reinhold Company.

Korzybski, Alfred. (1933). *Science and Sanity: An Introduction to Non-Aristotelian Systems and General Semantics.* Lancaster, PA: Science Press Printing Company.

Krannich, Ronald L. (1994). *Change Your Job, Change Your Life.* Manassas Park, VA: Impact Publications.

Kroeger, Otto, Thuesen, Janet M. (1992). *Type Talk at Work.* New York: Bantam Doubleday Dell Publishing Group, Inc.

Krol, Ed. (1994). *The Whole Internet.* Second Edition, Sebastopol, CA: O'Reilly & Associates.

Lewis, Adele, and Grappo, Gary J. (1993). How to Write Better Resumes. Hauppauge, NY: Barron's Educational Series.

Lewis, Michael. (2011). *Boomerang: travels in the new Third World.* New York and London: W.W.Norton & Company.

Lewis, Michael. (2010). *The Big Short.* New York and London: W.W.Norton & Company.

Likert, R. (1961). *New Patterns of Management.* New York: McGraw-Hill.

Lipman-Blumen, Jean. (1996). *Connective Edge.* San Francisco, CA: Jossey-Bass Publishers.

Liu, T. J., & Steele, C. M. (1986). Attribution as self-affirmation. *Journal of Personality and Social Psychology*, 51, 531-540.

Lock, R. (1988). *Job Search.* Pacific Grove: CA: Brooks Cole Publishing.

Lock, R. (1988). *Taking Charge of Your Career Direction.* Pacific Grove, CA: Brooks Cole Publishing.

London, Manuel. (1995). *Employees, Careers, and Job Creation.* San Francisco, CA: Jossey-Bass Publishers.

Ludden, L. (1998). *Job Savvy.* Indianapolis, IN: JIST Works, Inc.

Luft, Joseph. (1984). *The Johari Model, Group Process: An Introduction to Group Dynamics.* Mountain View, CA: Mayfield Publishing Company.

Martin L.R, Friedman H.S. (2000). Comparing personality scales across time: An illustrative study of validity and consistency in life-span archival data. *Journal of Personality.* 68, 85-110. [PubMed].

McDonald, James R. (1971). *Measurement of Differential Self-Perceptions of Supervisory and Subordinate Nursing Personnel.* Master's Thesis. [Google: McDonald Differential Perception of Nurses].

Mroczek, D.K., Almeida, D.M. (2004). The effects of daily stress, age, and personality on daily negative affect. *Journal of Personality.* 72:354-378.

Murphy, G. (1947). *Personality, a Biosocial Approach to Origins and Structure.* New York: Harper.

Murphy, K. (1991). *An Executive's Guide to Successful Job Hunting in Today's Tough Market.* New York: Bantam Books, Double Day Publishing.

Niles, S. G., Harris-Bowlsbey. (2002). *Career Development Interventions in the 21st Century.* Columbus, OH: Merrill Prentice Hall.

Norman P. Collins, S., Conner, M., Martin. R. (1995). *Attributions, Cognitions, and Coping Styles: Teleworkers' Reactions to Work-Related Problems. Journal of Applied Social Psychology*, 25, N(2), 117-128.

Pope, M. (2009). Jesse Buttrick Davis (1871-1955): Picture of vocational guidance in the schools. *Career Development Quarterly, 57, 278-288.*

Poulton, R. (2003*). Influence of life stress on depression: moderation by a polymorphism in the 5-HTT gene. *Science.* 301(5631):291-3. [PubMed].

Que Corporation. (1994). *Using the Internet.* Special Edition, Indianapolis, IN: Ewing, Publisher.

Reich, Robert B. (August 32, 1994). The Fracturing of the Middle Class. *New York Times*, page A19.

Scheier, M.F., Carver, C.S. (1985). Optimism, coping, and health: Assessment and implications of generalized outcome expectancies. *Health Psychology*, 4(3), 219-247.

Sedlar, J., Miners, R. (2007). *Don't Retire, Rewire.* New York: Alpha Books.

Shingleton, J. (1961). *Which Niches?* Holbrook, MA: Bob Adams, Inc., Publisher.

Sherman, D. K., & Cohen, G. L. (2006). The psychology of self-defense: Self-affirmation theory. In M. P. Zanna (Ed.) *Advances in Experimental Social Psychology* (Vol. 38, pp.183-242). San Diego, CA: Academic Press.

Sherman, D. K., & Cohen, G. L. (2002). Accepting threatening information: Self-affirmation and the reduction of defensive biases. *Current Directions in Psychological Science, 11, 119-123.*

Sherman, D. A. K., Nelson, L. D., & Steele, C. M. (2000). Do messages about health risks threaten the self? Increasing the acceptance of threatening health messages via self-affirmation. *Personality and Social Psychology Bulletin*, 26, 1046-1058.

Siegel, I. (1962). *Industrial Psychology.* Homewood, IL: Richard D. Irwin, Inc., Publisher.

Souverroff, V., Schmidt, D. (1992). *Break Through, Volumes One and Two.* Walnut Creek, CA: National Center for Career Change.

Stacey, C. L., DeMartino, M. F. (1958). *Understanding Human Motivation.* Cleveland, OH: Howard Allen, Inc., Publisher.

Steele, C. M. (1988). *The psychology of Self-affirmation: Sustaining the Integrity of the Self.* New York: Academic Press.

Strasser, S., Sena, J. (1990). *Successful Strategies from Mid-Career to Retirement.* Hawthorne, NJ: The Career Press.

Strutton, D., and Lumpkin J. (1992). Relationship Between Optimism and Coping Strategies in the Work Environment. *Psychological Reports, 71(3), 1179-1186.*

Super, D., Crites, J. (1962). *Appraising Vocational Fitness.* New York: Harper and Brothers.

Tesser, A., Cornell, D. P. (1991). On the confluence of self-processes. *Journal of Experimental Social Psychology, 27, 501-526.*

Walshok, M., Munroe, T., Devries, H. (2011). www. ClosingAmericasjobgap.com.

Wilson, Robert F., Rambusch, Eric, H. (1994). *Conquer Resume Objections.* New York: John Wiley and Sons, Inc.

Wing, Charles S. (1906). Reference to an early-published sermon: Story of the Engine that Thought It Could. *New York Tribune,* 8 April. (Wikipedia).

Yate, Martin (1992) Cover Letters that Knock' em Dead. Holbook, MA: Bob Adams, Inc.

Yate, Martin, (1993). *Resumes That knock' em Dead.* Holbook, MA: Bob Adams, Inc.

Zanna, P. (Ed.) *Advances in Experimental Social Psychology,* 38, 183-242. San Diego, CA: Academic

About the Author

Background

Jim McDonald's corporate human resources experience spans roughly forty years and include chemical process engineering, research and development, civil engineering, defense electronics, information systems, and construction management. He directed human resources for several large, San Francisco Bay Area companies, including FMC, Stanford Research Institute, Bechtel Engineering, Textron, and the URS Corporation.

In 1991, Jim formed his own firm and consulted over the next seven years to a variety f corporate and government clients, including the Navy and Air force.

As a consultant, Jim wrote two books, *a College Student's Guide to the World of Work*, followed by, *Managing Jobs and Careers in Transition*, written specifically for defense industry clients. In 2013, Jim published the first edition of, *Behavioral Strengths and Employment Strategies*.

Jim's perspective on occupational success is rooted in his own experience in managing employee and corporate change, particularly during periods of substantial economic growth and recession. Jim has extensive experience in corporate acquisitions and divestures, growth, outsourcing and transition. His experience spans the human resources life cycle, from employment to downsizing, from domestic to international compensation, from employee relations and unions to management training. Jim's experience provides a unique insight on how individual strengths and smart occupational strategies have led many to occupational success.

Education

Jim received a BA in Psychology and a MS in Industrial Psychology, from San Francisco State University. His thesis, *Measurement* of *Self-Perceptions of Supervisory and Subordinate Nursing Personnel*, was funded under a grant from the State of California.

Recognition

In 2007, the Northern California Human Resource Association, a chapter of the National Society for Human Resources Management (SHRM), recognized Jim as an Emeritus, for his leadership to NCHRA, and for his dedication to the field of Human Resources. Jim and his wife, Ann, reside in Castro Valley, CA.

∫∆ Integrating Change

Summary

Behavioral Strengths and Employment Strategies represents the author's "reverse engineering" of more than forty years of recruiting and employment management. The book describes career progression as the integration of two levels of self: the behavioral and the strategic. In the author's opinion, based on years of recruiting for a number of important corporations, occupational success is related to five self-strengths, and five practical employment strategies. **When used to reinforce each other, the five behavioral strengths and five employment strategies will result in life-long occupational success.**

Power of Self: Five Behavioral Dimensions

Optimism	Personality	Interests	Experience	Resilience
Positive outlook for future employment	Our internal and external image	Drive to explore, learn, and discover	Everything, work and otherwise	Capacity to overcome adversity and rejection

Occupational Solutions: Five Employment Strategies

Action	Research	Resumes	Interviews	Negotiation
From introspection to motion	Connecting interests and resources	Personality, interests, and experience	Meetings with employers, and others	Needs and Offers

- **Appendix A The Readiness Profile**

Using intuition and guesswork to guide one's career is the common approach, but career assessments work better. Similarly, the Career Readiness Profile (Appendix A) is designed to pull into focus one's preferred use of behavioral strengths and employment strategies.

- **Appendix B Twenty Answers to Twenty Tough Job Interview Questions**

Beyond the strategic use of positive career behaviors, answers to twenty tough interview questions **will give the applicant a tactical advantage over the interview pro**cess.

Appendix A

A Self-Directed Career Readiness Profile in 3 Steps

The Readiness Profile ©

A Self-Directed Strategy to Career Success

- **The Readiness Profile.** A Strategic Approach to Career Success

Using intuition and guess work to guide one's career is the common approach, but career assessments are much more effective. Most assessments are designed to help a user clarify important career behaviors and occupational strategies. Similarly, the Career Readiness Profile is designed to help clarify a user's view of their preferred use of positive career behaviors by asking the user to profile their agreement to a number of first-person behavioral and strategic career assertions.

Beyond the strategic use of positive career behaviors, the Career Readiness Profile suggests more specific, tactical ways of managing job and career success – the basis of career growth and development.

- **Your Profile is designed to answer four basic questions:**

1. **How strongly you agree with 50 first-person, positive career assertions.**
2. **Which of your behaviors and strategies you feel influence employers most.**
3. **Which behaviors and strategies you feel affect job success most.**
4. **Which strengths and strategies you feel are important for you to improve.**

A Self-Directed Career Profile from Three Directions

One Premise:

- **Individual Strengths lead to Occupational and Career Success**

The Readiness Profile rests on the assertion that we share the same universal behavioral strengths and use many of the same employment strategies to achieve occupational and career success.

Two Strengths:

- **Behavioral**
- **Strategic**

Job and career progression is approached using two kinds of strengths. The first, known as behavioral, consists of factors such as personality, interests, experience, resilience or sense of optimism. Our behavioral strengths are unique in that they operate mostly on auto pilot, until jarred by unexpected, emotional turmoil, such as sudden unemployment. The second type of strength represents our strategic approach to occupational and career progression. These strengths are centered on the use of five practical employment strategies, including motivation and action, research and discovery, marketing and resumes, interpersonal exchanges and interviews, and negotiating skills.

Three Insights:

- **Behavioral Assets**
- **Strategic Investments**
- **Occupational Growth**

Although occupational and career change never stand still, they can be measured. The Readiness Profile measures a user's position on career change from three vantage points:

1. **Your agreement ratings to fifty first-person assertions**
2. **The Behavioral and Occupational Strategies you feel influence employers most**
3. **The Behavioral and Occupational Strategies you feel are most important to occupational success**

Readiness Profile. Rate your Agreement to fifty career assertions, using a five-point scale, 1, 2, 3, 4, and 0, where a zero (0) rating means one is uncertain about their opinion toward the assertion, whereas, higher ratings (3 and 4) indicate a belief in the value or application of the assertion.

Sample Ratings, Factor One, Optimism.

Optimism Write your choice in the Score and Rating box	Strongly Disagree **1**	Disagree **2**	Agree **3**	Strongly Agree **4**	Uncertain **0**	Rating Score
1. I am optimistic that I will find new or better employment in the near future.			3			3
2. I feel optimistic about job referrals from friends and colleagues.				4		4
3. I stay in contact with my former employers for job leads.				4		4
4. I feel confident that my use of online social networks will help me find a job.		2				2
5. My sense of optimism has had a positive impact on my job search.					0	0
Transfer Total Rating to Summary Table Page 154						13

The five-point rating scale uses values from 1 (Strongly Disagree) to 4 (Strongly Agree), and 0, for Uncertain. Total ratings (1,2,3, 4, and 0) are totaled for each of the two Dimensions. Lower scores are affected by lower ratings (1 and 2), and "uncertain" ratings of "0."

Several exercises follow the rating Profile.

Exercise ① Rate your favored use of your Strengths and Strategies with employers

Exercise ② Rate your most important Strengths and Strategies used with employers

Exercise ③ Rate the Strengths and Strategies you feel important to improve

Turn page to begin the Profile ↓

Rating Matrix. **Optimism**

Optimism Write your score in both the Score and Rating box	Strongly Disagree **1**	Disagree **2**	Agree **3**	Strongly Agree **4**	Uncertain **0**	Rating Score
1.I am optimistic that I will find new or better employment in the near future.						
2. I feel optimistic about job referrals from friends and colleagues.						
3.I stay in contact with my former employers for job leads.						
4.I feel confident that my use of online social networks will help me find a job.						
5.My sense of optimism has had a positive impact on my job search.						
Transfer Total Rating to Summary Table Page 154						

Turn page to continue Profile ⬇

Rating Matrix. **Personality**

Personality Write your score in both the Score and Rating box	Strongly Disagree **1**	Disagree **2**	Agree **3**	Strongly Agree **4**	Uncertain **0**	Rating Score
6. I try to consider my personality when deciding what kinds of jobs to apply for.	☐	☐	☐	☐	☐	☐
7. I have taken several personality tests to better understand which jobs I'm suited for.	☐	☐	☐	☐	☐	☐
8. I use the force of my personality to get my point across to others.	☐	☐	☐	☐	☐	☐
9. I know how my personality comes across to others.	☐	☐	☐	☐	☐	☐
10. I understand the kinds of managerial styles that best fit my personality.	☐	☐	☐	☐	☐	☐
Transfer Total Rating to Summary Table Page 154						☐

Turn page to continue Profile ↓

Rating Matrix. **Interests**

Interests Write your score in both the Score and Rating box	Strongly Disagree **1**	Disagree **2**	Agree **3**	Strongly Agree **4**	Uncertain **0**	Rating Score
11. I have a good sense of the kinds of jobs that match my long-term interests.	☐	☐	☐	☐	☐	☐
12. I have taken several career inventories to get a better idea of which jobs suit my interests.	☐	☐	☐	☐	☐	☐
13. I know the kinds of jobs that match my immediate career interests.	☐	☐	☐	☐	☐	☐
14. I clearly know the kinds of jobs I would like to pursue.	☐	☐	☐	☐	☐	☐
15. I'm passionate about staying in my current industry.	☐	☐	☐	☐	☐	☐
Transfer Total Rating to Summary Table Page 154						☐

Turn page to continue Profile ↓

Rating Matrix. **Experience**

Experience Write your score in both the Score and Rating box	Strongly Disagree **1**	Disagree **2**	Agree **3**	Strongly Agree **4**	Uncertain **0**	Rating Score
16. My experience is relevant to today's job market.	☐	☐	☐	☐	☐	☐
17. I have substantial related work experience and education in my chosen career field.	☐	☐	☐	☐	☐	☐
18. I frequently take classes that enhance my skill set.	☐	☐	☐	☐	☐	☐
19. I frequently undertake new projects and challenges in my workplace.	☐	☐	☐	☐	☐	☐
20. I learn new technologies in order to adapt to my work environment.	☐	☐	☐	☐	☐	☐
Transfer Total Rating to Summary Table Page 154						☐

Turn page to continue Profile ↓

Rating Matrix. **Resilience**

Resilience Write your score in both the Score and Rating box	Strongly Disagree **1**	Disagree **2**	Agree **3**	Strongly Agree **4**	Uncertain **0**	Rating Score
21. My self-confidence and sense of self-worth help me cope with employer rejections.	☐	☐	☐	☐	☐	☐
22. I remain positive even under the pressure of a stressful interview.	☐	☐	☐	☐	☐	☐
23. I am able to retain my sense of self-worth in spite of extended unemployment.	☐	☐	☐	☐	☐	☐
24. I am persistent in my job search even though it's sometimes discouraged.	☐	☐	☐	☐	☐	☐
25. I can overcome challenging situations and tasks.	☐	☐	☐	☐	☐	☐
Transfer Total Rating to Summary Table Page 154						☐

Turn page to continue Profile ↓

Rating Matrix. **Action**

Action Write your score in both the Score and Rating box	Strongly Disagree **1**	Disagree **2**	Agree **3**	Strongly Agree **4**	Uncertain **0**	Rating Score
26. I am taking positive steps to get that next job.	☐	☐	☐	☐	☐	☐
27. I have taken steps to improve my communication skills.	☐	☐	☐	☐	☐	☐
28. I have written a job search plan that I am putting into action.	☐	☐	☐	☐	☐	☐
29. I have developed a wide network of contacts in my industry.	☐	☐	☐	☐	☐	☐
30. My plans and actions are generating promising employer contacts.	☐	☐	☐	☐	☐	☐
Transfer Total Rating to Summary Table Page 154						☐

Turn page to continue Profile ↓

Rating Matrix. **Research**

Research Write your score in both the Score and Rating box	Strongly Disagree 1	Disagree 2	Agree 3	Strongly Agree 4	Uncertain 0	Rating Score
31. I regularly use the Internet to research jobs, companies, and career resources.	☐	☐	☐	☐	☐	☐
32. I often search for jobs on job boards, such as Indeed and CareerBuilder.	☐	☐	☐	☐	☐	☐
33. I regularly use Boolean techniques to search the Internet.	☐	☐	☐	☐	☐	☐
34. I use library databases to find industry managers and leaders.	☐	☐	☐	☐	☐	☐
35. I read articles and reports about my industry and employment trends.	☐	☐	☐	☐	☐	☐
Transfer Total Rating to Summary Table Page 154						☐

Turn page to continue Profile ↓

Rating Matrix. **Resumes**

Resumes Write your score in both the Score and Rating box	Strongly Disagree 1	Disagree 2	Agree 3	Strongly Agree 4	Uncertain 0	Rating Score
36. My resume includes a brief summary of my work contributions, interests, and experience.	☐	☐	☐	☐	☐	☐
37. I have updated my resume to reflect my most recent education and training.	☐	☐	☐	☐	☐	☐
38. I regularly update my resume to reflect my current experience.	☐	☐	☐	☐	☐	☐
39. I emphasize work contributions with the use of action words and quantifiable results.	☐	☐	☐	☐	☐	☐
40. My resume reflects a clear connection to the jobs I am seeking.	☐	☐	☐	☐	☐	☐
Transfer Total Rating to Summary Table Page 154						☐

Turn page to continue Profile ↓

Rating Matrix. **Interviews**

Interviews Write your score in both the Score and Rating box	Strongly Disagree **1**	Disagree **2**	Agree **3**	Strongly Agree **4**	Uncertain **0**	Rating Score
41. I am comfortable interviewing for a job.	☐	☐	☐	☐	☐	☐
42. I find it helpful to underline key features of the job opening before interviewing.	☐	☐	☐	☐	☐	☐
43. I have interviewed for several jobs where I felt in control of the process.	☐	☐	☐	☐	☐	☐
44. I feel confident using interview strategies such as asking to clarify job responsibilities.	☐	☐	☐	☐	☐	☐
45. I can easily communicate my strengths and special talents.	☐	☐	☐	☐	☐	☐
Transfer Total Rating to Summary Table Page 154						☐

Turn page to continue Profile ↓

Rating Matrix. **Negotiations**

Negotiations Write your score in both the Score and Rating box	Strongly Disagree **1**	Disagree **2**	Agree **3**	Strongly Agree **4**	Uncertain **0**	Rating Score
46. I can negotiate the terms and conditions of a job offer.						
47. Before negotiating, I have a clear picture of what I need in salary and benefits.						
48. I make sure a job offer is in writing to avoid misunderstandings.						
49. I try to be the first to determine what the manager feels is the ideal offer before stating my salary expectations.						
50. I have the communication skills and confidence to negotiate a job offer.						
Transfer Total Rating to Summary Table Page 154						

Turn page to Profile Summary Rating Table and Exercises ⬇

A Career Readiness Profile in 3 Steps

Profile Table

Your Total Ratings for each Factor

Optimism	Personality	Interests	Experience	Resilience	Strengths
Page 144	Page 145	Page 146	Page 147	Page 148	Total Ratings
Action	Research	Resumes	Interviewing	Negotiating	Strategies
					Total Ratings
Page 149	Page 150	Page 151	Page 152	Page 153	

Understanding total Scores

From the Profile Table above, check x the box below that corresponds to your total Ratings for Strengths, and for Strategies.

☐	1 to 25	*Strongly Disagree with Strengths Assertions*
☐	26 to 50	*Mostly Disagree with Strengths Assertions*
☐	51 to 75	*Mostly Agree with Strengths Assertions*
☐	76 to 100	*Substantially Agree with Strengths Assertions*

☐	1 to 25	*Strongly Disagree with Strategies Assertions*
☐	26 to 50	*Mostly Disagree with Strategies Assertions*
☐	51 to 75	*Mostly Agree with Strategies Assertions*
☐	76 to 100	*Substantially Agree with Strategies Assertions*

Question. Are your Scores higher for Strengths than Strategies? Vice Versa?

Turn page to continue Profile Exercises

Pen or pencil in your selections with a ● or ✓.

Exercise ① Which Behavioral Strengths and Employment Strategies do you use most when pursuing employment?

Behavioral Strengths	Behaviors you use Most when pursuing employment
Optimism	O
Personality	O
Interests	O
Experience	O
Resilience	O

Employment Strategies	Strategies you use Most when pursuing employment
Action	O
Research	O
Resumes	O
Interviewing	O
Negotiating	O

Exercise ② In general, which Behavioral Strengths and Employment Strategies do you consider the most effective means of influencing employers?

Behavioral Strengths	Most Effective Behaviors
Optimism	O
Personality	O
Interests	O
Experience	O
Resilience	O

Employment Strategies	Most Effective Strategies
Action	O
Research	O
Resumes	O
Interviewing	O
Negotiating	O

Exercise ③ Which Behaviors and Strategies do you plan to improve?

Behavioral Strengths	Most Important Behaviors
Optimism	O
Personality	O
Interests	O
Experience	O
Resilience	O

Employment Strategies	Most Important Strategies
Action	O
Research	O
Resumes	O
Interviewing	O
Negotiating	O

Turn Page for a Recap of your Readiness Profile ↓

Profile Recap

Begin with the assertion that we are all capable of improving.

The Readiness Profile represents what you feel influences employers most, from use of the strengths of your personality and sense of optimism to your resume and interviewing skills.

- Your Profile is designed to answer four basic questions:

1. **How strongly you agree with 50 self-described positive career strengths and strategies.**
2. **Which of your behaviors and strategies you feel influence employers most.**
3. **Which behaviors and strategies you feel affect job success most.**
4. **Which strengths and strategies you feel are important for to improve.**

Depending on how confident you feel with your current strengths and strategies, you have a least three options going forward:

- Continue using the same strengths and strategies you feel confident will result in job and career success.

- Strengthen your job coping skills by developing lesser used strengths and strategies scored 10 or less on one or more of the five Factors.

- Continue to research the Internet, self-help groups, dedicated non-profit resources, or from career coaches. With their help, it may take only an hour or so of your time to get a feel for a new, wonderful career direction.

Final Note: Your Profile of strengths and strategies is a snapshot of what you consider important to you, today. Therefore, use your Profile as a guide to future occupations and careers. In the meantime, all the best for continued success.

∫Δ *Integrating Change*

Appendix B

Twenty Answers to Twenty Tough Job Interview Questions

Appendix B

Twenty Answers to Twenty Tough Job Interview Questions

Job interviews are designed to reveal four basic facets of an applicant: personality, interests, experience, and commitment.

Although job interviews have one basic purpose: the interview process, on the other hand, come in an infinite variety of forms, from open-ended and unstructured, to precisely scripted and choreographed. Some interviewers do most of the talking, whereas others use a set of structured, behavioral questions. Occasionally, an interviewer will struggle with their own inexperience, whereas, other interviewers will use the interview process to "drill below the surface," trying to snag contradictions and inconsistencies. Luckily, most interviewers follow a set of questions that are framed to explore an applicant's ability to perform the job. In most cases, job **interviews will follow four, rather distinct phases.**

Four Phases of a Job Interview

I Personality	communication style, character, temperament
II Interests	rationale for applying
III Experience	job history, credibility
IV Resolution	negotiating job offer

Unlike the statistical bell-shaped curve, the actual distribution of interview questions will depend largely on a manager's assessment of the applicant's qualifications. For example, managers in research and engineering, almost always concentrate on an applicant's technical experience and problem solving. On the other hand, retail sales and marketing will often emphasize questions that explore an applicant's personality and interpersonal skills.

The final phase in a job interview often tests an applicant's interest in joining the company. If the signals are mutually positive, the manger and applicant will engage in mutual bargaining over the employer's offer of "terms and conditions," such as pay and or benefits, up to an actual offer.

At each phase of the interview, from Personality to Resolution, be prepared to answer tough questions, such as the twenty cited on the following pages. Write down the number of the question that you feel you need to practice.

The Bell-shaped Curve of Job Interview

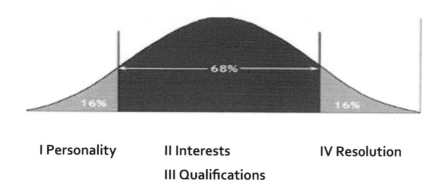

I Personality   II Interests   IV Resolution

III Qualifications

The actual amount of time allocated to the four phases **is a theoretical distribution**. In realty, most interviewers concentrate on uncovering an applicant's job experience and qualifications. **Whereas one interviewer may concentrate questions on the applicant's job experience, another interviewer will explore an applicant's personality. In most cases, though, an interviewer will use questions that determine the applicant's qualifications for the job.**

In spite of the universe of interview questions, a few are known to be tough to answer. Let's start with the first phase of tough questions.

Phase I Questions dealing with an applicant's, interpersonal style, character, temperament

---

1 **"Tell me a little about yourself."** (So easy to ask, so difficult to answer!)

One of the first questions asked is intended to find out a little about the applicant. The question is friendly, inviting and nerve rattling. The answer is known to book authors as their elevator pitch: short, concise, to the point. A sample response for an engineering applicant might go something like,

"I' have recently separated from XYZ, after ten years as a design engineer. I was recently promoted to a system engineer, but my real interests are in software engineering. To help me prepare for my next job, I have recently completed 30 units of software engineering classes."

Several things are accomplished by this question. Most importantly, it is an icebreaker. The question sounds friendly and innocent-enough, but, even if you don't realize it, the **answer indicates how well one can handle vague, open-ended situations.**

Note the ending comment, "30 units of software" classes, opens the door to more questions on education. Given the last thought points to education, there is a good chance the interviewer will follow with a question dealing with education. For example, the interviewer may ask you what specific classes you have taken. Generally, what topic or subject you choose to end your comment with often leads the interviewers into their next question. In fact, the, "tell me a little about yourself" question may be one of the few places where an applicant may have some control over the direction of the interview.

With a brief reference to current work history out of the way (high interest to the interviewer), continue with any educational accomplishments, mentioning a few major work contributions. Limit your answer to no more than 2 to 3 minutes. The following is another sample response to the question:

"After graduate school in business, I worked for a small retail book store chain. I implemented a PC-based accounting system which saved each store about 25 hours per week of owner's time. I continued that job for two years until joining a national non-profit organization, dealing with the hearing impaired. I can go into more detail if you wish, but that pretty much brings my work history up to date."

Note that the applicant's ending reference to a "national non-profit organization" should elicit questions that explore in more detail the applicant's responsibilities and contributions.

Personality: style, character, temperament

---

4. "Aside from your general background, in what ways do you consider yourself unique?"

Like your resume, no two people are alike when it comes to blending skills, experience, academic achievements, interests, and personality.

For a person with little work experience, combining a third-party compliment ("I've been told by others...") with a personal contribution or two will help establish a sense of who you are with the interviewer.

In your own words, use something like the following:

"Without a lot of experience it is a little difficult to cite specific work skills, but I've been told by several of my friends at school that I have very good communication skills. My Young Leaders

role in church has taught me a good deal about problem conflict resolution, and the importance of listening effectively."

Personality: style, character, temperament

---

16. "What would this job mean to you?"

This question reflects an important aspect of any job. That is, the job's intrinsic worth and not just its monetary value. For example, a receptionist applicant who has all the requisite job skills, but is, admittedly, painfully shy, may see the job as an opportunity to improve interpersonal skills and self-confidence with the public. A sample answer might follow with something like:

"The receptionist position represents a chance for me to interact with a lot of people. I am very shy around strangers but I think the job as receptionist would help me greatly to overcome my bashfulness."

Personality: style, character, temperament

9, "As long as we are on the subject of management, how would you describe your leadership style?"

The questions apply to more than those seeking a supervisory position. Virtually all of us will respond to the question, in one way or another. The interviewer may have an interest in those with potential supervisory skills. You might research "management practices or topics on leadership styles. If the question is presented, have some idea how others might characterize your leadership style.

There are a number of ways to answer the question, if it gets thrown your way, but the following example can be put into your own words.

Whenever I can I try to delegate responsibility, taking into account the abilities and desires of my team. No manger is perfect, but I try to encourage initiative and growth. I try to be mindful of reasonable and attainable goals. I make it a point to recognize contributions and progress.

Personality: style, character, temperament

---

10. "How have you handled personal disappointments at work?"

Personal disappoints and setbacks are common in the workplace. They vary from unfair assignments to lack of promotions and advancement. Bouncing back from personal setbacks and workplace conflict is a sign of maturity and resilience - two attributes manager's look for in their subordinates. Although not a common question, it is intended to measure an applicant's ability to handle unpleasant change. How to answer the question takes some inner reflection.

I guess we all feel left out at times. It's common. I try to stay connected with those I work with, but will discuss my feelings with my manager if I think the problem is serious. Luckily, my sense of optimism and resilience helps me get over minor personal disappointments. I try to remain flexible and, at the same time, keep things in perspective.

Phase II Questions dealing with an Applicant's career Interests

---

5. "Given your interests, what kind of jobs are you concentrating on?"

"I'm experienced in manufacturing operations, but my ultimate aim is to use my course work in accounting to obtain a position in accounts payable or receivable."

Under some circumstances, the interview may not involve a specific job. The interviewer's question may be, *"What kind of jobs have you been looking for?"* One response to this question could be something like:

"Right now I am concentrating less on any specific position, but more on certain industries, like the one your company is involved in."

Career Interests

---

12 "Why (have you) are you leaving your present job?"

"I have just finished working to progress technically and want to use my interest in management for a company in your industry."

Or, "*I am seeking a position where my experience* (*interest, initiative, drive, motivation, fervor; use the adjective that you feel most comfortable with*) *can be used by a rapidly growing company.*"

One person suggested the following:

"*Although I feel comfortable in my current job, I am interested in working for a company where I can develop additional management experience.*"

Sometimes, one answer will logically lead to another, such as the following: "*Did you look for opportunities within your current company?*" Be prepared with a possible answer, but don't volunteer an answer unless asked. If you are or have left a company, stay away from blaming others for your having left. "The place was a zoo," has rarely convinced any interviewer. Criticizing one's prior boss, co-workers, or company, justified or not, will likely create an impression that you are the source of the complaint, and not others.

Practice a few times with the wording until you are comfortable with your answer.

Career Interests

13. "How you would you describe your ideal job?"

This open-ended question is designed to compare your expectations with what the company has to offer. Explain that your ideal job is one that encourages improvement, offers training and opportunities to make a difference to a department's success.

14. "Why do you think your background **might add value to this company?**

Applicants tend to "halo" or gloss over this question with something like,

"*I have heard about the company and it sounds like a great good place to work.*"

Your compliment may be sincere but may come across as shallow unless you back it up with something like an employee recommendation. If you cannot refer to an employee, back up your interest and credibility in the company with knowledge about the company. Conduct a thorough online search of the company. Call the company marketing division for an Annual Report. Ask for sales, or product information. All of these things will help you gain a better insight into the company's missions, values and appeal. If you know the company and feel comfortable with the product line, the above question could be answered with something like:

"Although there are a number of companies like yours in this industry, from what I have learned so far is that your company is one of the leaders in the field."

Suggest that you have researched the company, or that you have friends that work for the company, Make sure you fee; strongly about contributing to the company's on-going success,

Phase III Questions dealing with an Applicant's Job Experience and Credibility

7. "In what ways have you been able to make contributions to your jobs?"

This question offers a great opportunity to cite improvements you feel were important to your job. Cite specific examples, such as training others, working on special projects or accepting additional responsibilities. Describe how your contributions made a difference to the success of the team. One client has offered the following answer to the previous question:

"Because I worked in a start-up, we were constantly challenged to come up with new ways of solving problems and creating value for our customers. That is the same kind of environment I am seeking."

Job Experience and Credibility

6. "What did you like best about your previous bosses?"

"I learned that no single management style guarantees success. I think it is more important to adjust to different management styles." This answer is a lot better than saying, "I figured out how to handle my boss who was a real jerk."

A number of readers have pointed out that something positive can be found in almost any job, or supervisor. When the question about what you liked best about your previous bosses, point out one or more positive attributes. There are some exceptions, but point out how your boss encouraged more training and development. Most bosses leave a positive mark, even if is small.

Job Experience and Credibility

---

15. "Now that you know a little about the position, what is your impression?" (Here is your chance to think before responding.)

From what can recall during the interview, or from notes, rephrase the three to four most important job responsibilities. Convey your understanding of the job and its importance to others, inside and outside the company. For example, one might say something like,

"From my understanding, it appears the position requires a good deal of unsupervised initiative, teamwork, and customer service skills."

If appropriate, stress the need for good communications, or physical stamina. This is one question where notes come in handy.

Job Experience and Credibility

---

2. "What do you consider your strongest skills?"

Another typical but tough question. If you have an idea about what kinds of skills the employer may be looking for, then gear your response to their questions. We all have a number of strengths, some greater than others.

Weaknesses are relative. A weakness under one circumstance may be strength in another. A five-foot teenager against college basketball players is at a disadvantage, but possibly a real asset to the high school junior varsity basketball team. The same goes for occupational strengths, they are relative to the job opening.

If you don't know for sure what kinds of specific skills are needed for the job, cite a couple of your transferable skills, such as communications, or problem solving. Conclude your answer by citing several other specific skills you possess that are related to the job opening.

Job Experience and Credibility

> **3. "On the flip side, what do you consider your weaker skills, and what have you done to improve them?"**

A sample response might be something like the following: ˙

"Because of my need for perfection [relative weakness], my reports have occasionally put me behind schedule. I now realize that my excessive need for perfection has caused some delays. But, in the last year or so, I've been able to balance my need for detail with the company's need for timely reports."

Be prepared to talk about a weakness you have overcome. For example, after citing a weaker skill, go on to explain what steps you have taken to overcome the deficiency. A weakness in computer skills, for example, can be overcome by taking computer science classes. **Working to overcome areas of weakness is generally viewed by managers to be a wonderful trait.** Most managers feel that applicants who are concerned with personal improvement will, in all likelihood, work on job performance as well.

Job Experience and Credibility

> **8.** Once in a while the interviewer may ask, **"In what ways did your manager promote team work?"**

The interviewer may be interested in your attitude toward certain styles of leadership and team work. Personality behaviors, like "control," can cause the applicant to display favorable or negative non-verbal signals. Consider your answer before answering this question. However, if pushed, keep your response positive.

If appropriate, emphasize the benefits of team work. Focus on positive outcomes with past or current supervisors and co-workers. If appropriate, briefly describe how your supervisor improved team performance, or encouraged initiative or recognized special contributions.

Phase IV Resolution: exchanging qualifications for a job offer

---

17. "What kind of a salary are you looking for?"

Why should you delay answering questions about salary? Because you're negotiating position improves the more you know about job requirements and responsibilities. Also, salary is a quick but superficial way for the interviewer to screen candidates out of the applicant pool.

Why not just ask for the interviewer for the salary? If the salary is less than you are looking for what then do you do.? Excuse yourself from the meeting? What if the salary cited by the interviewer is higher than your salary? Again, the question leads back to job expectations and responsibilities. In some way, the differences have to be explained.

This is a tough question, for two reasons. It s rare for an applicant to know much, if anything about the employer's salary ranges, or the salary range for the job one is applying for. Secondly, without a good idea what job duties and responsibilities are required, a precise answer to the salary question will be a shot in the dark. If you don't have the employer's salary information at hand, and if pushed by the interviewer for your salary, you could answer with something like the following:

"I wish I could be more specific about what salary I am looking for, but before I can give you an intelligent answer, I honestly feel I need to know more about the job and the salary you have in mind for the job. However, I am accustomed to a base annual salary of roughly ....."

Another approach to the salary question might to go something like:

"I am accustomed to making between $X and $Y......, but, frankly, I am more interested in compensation commensurate with the job and with others in similar positions."

And, one could add nuance to the interviewer's question with something like:

"I'm currently paid $$ per year, not counting other company contributions. Although I feel I am adequately paid at this point in my career, I feel the chance to assume greater responsibility is more important to me than an increase in compensation."

Exchanging qualifications for a job offer

> **19. "In retrospect, I am not sure where we can fit your background to this job opening? This job requires a different level of experience."**

Rejecting an applicant who is over or under qualified is relative; in other words, qualified is in the eye of the interviewer. Whether over or under qualified, this classic rejection offers the applicant an opportunity to negotiate their image. Your answer provides a perfect time to negotiate the mindset of the interviewer. **Convincing a manager that being over qualified means being able to hit the ground running, may cause the interviewer to see you differently.** Likewise, insufficient experience means an opportunity to dedicate your energy over and above what would normally be expected - another positive image maker. **In any event, treat a denial as an opportunity to negotiate an improved image in the eyes of the interviewer.**

Exchanging qualifications for a job offer

> **20. "Do you have any final questions?"**

The interviewer may apologize for asking so many questions, and may turn to you, out of courtesy, to give you a chance to ask some questions. Consider this a great opportunity to leverage your qualifications with several good questions for the interviewer.

Make sure you have a few questions intended to clarify key responsibilities of the job. Stay away from questions concerning benefits and compensation. It is better to wait until the interviewer raises the possibility of an offer before requesting information on benefits and compensation. Questions about compensation and benefits are typically raised after a job offer has been alluded to or after a job has been offered.

Exchanging qualifications for a job offer

After completing the formal portion of the interview, restate your interest in the job, Even if the "signals" are negative, respond with something like the following:

""I remain impressed with the things we talked about. If appropriate, I would welcome an opportunity to meet with others on your team?"

An expression of interest in pursuing employment will force a decisive, "go, no go," from the manager. If the interviewer is unsure of an applicant's qualifications they will likely defer answering the "next step" question by explaining that they need to interview other candidates. This may be true, but the explanation is often a delay tactic.

Again, express appreciation for the opportunity to meet. Tell the interviewer you look forward to meeting again. If the manager does not call within a week, leave a follow-up message. If you still get no response, move onto your next opportunity.

Index

A

Action 7, 8, 10, 13, 19, 30, 31, 43, 45, 51, 52, 53, 54, 55, 57, 59, 68, 85, 88, 89, 90, 91, 92, 93, 94, 97, 129

Ads 41, 55, 57, 61, 64, 65, 66, 68, 87, 100, 102, 103

Adversity 7, 8, 20, 49, 51, 52, 55, 68

Applicant Management Systems (AMS) 80, 96, 97

Aptitudes 26, 42, 44

Attire 53, 57, 103, 106

B

Behavioral Strength 48, 49, 50

Benefits 19, 20, 25, 34, 36, 40, 45, 63, 66, 67, 68, 70, 76, 78, 112, 115, 117, 118, 119, 121, 123, 158, 166, 168

Biosocial Theory 22

Building Optimism 18

Business Associations 63

C

Career Interests 32, 37, 162, 163

Change 5, 8, 11, 12, 13, 16, 18, 19, 20, 23, 28, 31, 32, 33, 36, 37, 38, 39, 42, 43, 45, 46, 47, 49, 50, 52, 53, 55, 59, 60, 62, 68, 74, 75, 80, 85, 109, 117, 122, 123, 128, 129, 130, 132, 135, 162

Communications 15, 17, 19, 24, 25, 28, 29, 36, 40, 41, 44, 54, 55, 56, 57, 59, 61, 63, 66, 71, 76, 78, 87, 88, 92, 99, 100, 102, 106, 111, 113, 114, 116, 125, 158, 161, 165

Community Sanctuaries 62

Competencies 26

Competing Offers 121

Confirmation 111, 125

Contacts 14, 15, 16, 17, 19, 45, 53, 56, 57, 59, 60, 61, 62, 63, 64, 67, 71, 81, 86, 99, 109, 116, 126

Contingency 67

Contributions 3, 8, 19, 40, 41, 63, 85, 87, 88, 89, 90, 91, 92, 107, 112, 120, 121, 160, 162, 164, 167

Contributions that Speak 90

Credibility 16, 91, 98, 99, 101, 106, 107, 109, 158, 164, 165, 166